HAUNTED HIGHWAYS

Dan Asfar

GHOST HOUSE

Ghost House Books

The Publisher: Ghost House Books
Distributed by Lone Pine Publishing

10145 – 81 Avenue   1808 B Street NW, Suite 140
Edmonton, AB T6E 1W9   Auburn, WA
Canada   USA 98001

Website: http://www.ghostbooks.net

National Library of Canada Cataloguing in Publication Data

Asfar, Dan, 1973–
  Haunted highways / Dan Asfar.

  ISBN 1–894877–29–2

  1. Ghosts. 2. Haunted places. 3. Roads—Folklore. I. Title.
BF1461.A83 2003   133.1'22   C2002–911490–X

Editorial Director: Nancy Foulds
Project Editor: C.D. Wangler
Proofreading: Dori Anne Blackie
Illustrations Coordinator: Carol Woo
Production Manager: Gene Longson
Cover Design: Gerry Dotto
Layout & Production: Jeff Fedorkiw

Photo Credits: Every effort has been made to accurately credit photographers. Any errors or omissions should be directed to the publisher for changes in future editions. The photographs in this book are reproduced with the kind permission of the following sources: Glenbow Archives, Calgary, Canada (p. 14: NA-5634-3); Rick Riedel and TravDestRevue.com (p. 25); Dee Marie Freedman, Hauntings Research Group (p. 29); Lynett McKell (p. 53); Gettysburg Online, www.gettysburgbattlefieldonline.com (p. 69, 92, 95); *A Complete History of Lives and Robberies of the Most Notorious Highwaymen* by Alexander Smith (1719) (p. 151); National Archives, Still Pictures Branch (p. 197: NWDNS-111-B-1905); Chicago Historical Society (p. 223: DN-0087707); Eastland Disaster Historical Society, (877) 865-6295, www.eastlanddisaster.org (p. 216); Corbis Images (p. 3, 4-5, 11, 32, 43, 116, 183); Library of Congress (p. 73: HAER,P,9-PIPERV,3-3; p. 99: HAER,P,9-PIPERV,3-1; p. 119: USZ62-099093; p. 124: HABS,PA,23-RAD,1B-1; p. 127: USZ62-117931; p. 135: USZ62-108487; p. 141: D4-34895; p. 180: USF33-T01-001270-M3; p. 190: USZ62-4350; p. 200: B8171-1287; p. 206: USF34-051588-D; p. 209: USF34-051361-D; p. 221: USZ62-108487).

The stories, folklore and legends in this book are based on the author's collection of sources including individuals whose experiences have led them to believe they have encountered phenomena of some kind or another. They are meant to entertain, and neither the publisher nor the author claims these stories represent fact.

We acknowledge the financial support of the Government of Canada through the Book Publishing Industry Development Program (BPIDP) for our publishing activities.

PC: 06

For E.M.

CONTENTS

Chapter Four: Historic Thoroughfares

Chapter Five: Haunted Streets and Roads

Acknowledgments

All the stories in this book are based on purported haunt-ings on roads across the United States, Canada and the United Kingdom. Although most of these accounts are well known in their respective regions, none of them would have been presented as well as they are in this book if it weren't for the talented staff at Ghost House Books. My thanks to Shane Kennedy and Nancy Foulds for their continued faith and confidence. I'd also like to acknowl-edge Carol Woo for her efforts in tracking down the pho-tographs in this work, and Jeff Fedorkiw for giving the book its form. I also appreciate the efforts of researcher Alana Bevan in digging up so many of the ghost stories in this book, and of course my editor, Chris Wangler, for his insight, his humor and his editorial eye. Thanks all.

Introduction

I can't say if it was a case of too much Jack Kerouac, too much Tom Waits or too little sense, but a good chunk of my early adulthood was spent on the road. Cursed with a chronic case of itchy feet during my late teens and early twenties, I spent a lot of time walking along the shoulders of highways with nothing but a backpack, a few bucks and a hopeful thumb jutting into traffic. Inevitably, more than one sun set before I found a ride, leaving me to make the best bed I could on the side of the road. I can remember pitching my tent a stone's throw away from a major highway in southwest France just as a storm was beginning to gather, falling asleep to the sound of pouring rain and car tires hissing on wet asphalt. Another night in Mayo County, Ireland, the full moon lit up the narrow, desolate road I had just hitched up, and the surrounding bog shone silver as the wind roared over the Atlantic Ocean, which crashed into the cliffs below. There were other times, in other places, where it was only me, the road and the cars. And while I was often struck by the sight of a highway stretching over a foreign land, I can honestly say that I never felt a twang of anything that resembled fear.

That was until May 2001. My girlfriend and I were on a road trip, returning home after driving down the west coast to Los Angeles. We were in southern Utah at the time, driving along the I15 in the direction of Zion National Park, where we planned to spend a little time scrabbling over the red rock the following day. The sun had set when we reached the Highway 9 turnoff to the park, and by the time we were in Zion, it was pitch black.

Until then, my passenger and I hadn't given nighttime travel much thought; neither of us had any particular aversion to the dark, and we had driven late into the night a few times in California without any problems. Sure, setting up camp in the dark was a bit of a pain, but it was only a minor inconvenience. The troubles on this drive, however, were of an entirely different nature.

The feeling set in shortly after we passed the town of Hurricane on Highway 9. Both of us became quiet as we looked out at the road ahead of us. It was dark; the surrounding desert was practically invisible, and besides the dim orange light coming from the town, which was rapidly disappearing behind us, the only thing we could see was the narrow strip of highway illuminated by the car headlights.

We were in the park about half an hour later, being tenuously guided towards the campground by periodic road signs that suddenly appeared out of the darkness. Outside, we could make out the vague shapes of the massive rock formations looming around us; a fierce wind was blowing over the park. "Where is this campground already?" my girlfriend asked from the passenger side, staring at the darkness around us.

"It has to be coming up soon," I said, trying to ignore the growing anxiety. I guess my voice belied my efforts, because she looked at me uncomfortably.

"This road is creeping me out," she said.

"Yeah, me too."

"I don't know what it is."

I tried to lighten the mood. "It reminds me of this one ghost story," I began.

Her response was quick and tinged with more than a little irritation. "Not now."

I know this is going to sound anticlimactic, but that was it. We eventually found our campsite, set up our tent in the blustering desert wind and cooked up a late-night dinner before retiring. We consciously blocked out the eeriness of the ride into the park. I guess it doesn't seem like much now. There were no dramatic apparitions, flashes of light or disembodied sounds. No phantom truck roared past us, and a mangled ghostly hitchhiker did not suddenly appear by the side of the road. But that night, while we drove into Zion, some part of me almost expected that there would be.

The open road. It looms large in the North American ethos, where mobility has often been a byword for freedom, and distant horizons are opportunities waiting to be discovered. A place in-between places, a channel to the outside world, a moving vantage point for the surrounding countryside—highways can be described in many different ways. For those restless drifters unable to settle down, highways are even called home.

Not that the unsettled souls drifting over the continent's byways are the only ones who have made highways into dwelling places. There are others—the spirits, beasts, visions and victims who seem to be trapped in the perpetual transience of the road. These are the ghosts of the highway, neither leaving nor arriving, neither living nor dead, but languishing in a state somewhere between, reliving past tragedies, fatalities and obsessions in front of those unfortunate enough to see them. They are the mysterious beasts that stalk rural thoroughfares, creatures never classified by any phylum, genus or species, lurking along the backroads of the country's heartland; they terrorize locals and motorists alike. They are also the inexplicable lights that continue to flash across North American roads, from Ontario to Ohio, Michigan to Texas, revealing some mystery from the past to crowds of enthralled and terrified spectators.

There is an entire genre of ghost lore set on the highways, byways, bridges and roads of North America and elsewhere. Whether they are phantom hitchhikers stealing rides with motorists, long-dead criminals haunting the bridges they were hanged on or the victims of car accidents who hover over the roads that claimed them, sightings of spirits on the road are abundant. Some are centuries old, dating back to times when people got around on horseback, while others find their roots in recent decades, the products of horrific car accidents that have left supernatural scars on infamous stretches of road. To this day, these haunted passages remind us all that there is more to the world than meets the eye, and not all roads lead to Rome.

1
Lights
on the Road

Moving orbs of light number among the most frequently reported supernatural phenomena on North American highways. They hover over lonely roads, dart across bridges and slowly make their way to unknown destinations. Although most of them remain visible for only a few minutes before vanishing into the darkness, the impact these lights have on the surrounding community is always significant. The lights are usually accompanied by a legend that reaches back to a forgotten tragedy on the road. As a result, it has become something of a supernatural truism that wherever highway lights appear, so too does death.

The Elmore Bridge

On March 21, 1919, a young man named Billy O'Rielly sped across northern Ohio along scenic Highway 105, moving fast beside the Portage River. He sat atop his brand-new Indian Motorcycle, celebrating his new lease on life with a wide-open throttle and an open road. Billy had spent the better part of the previous year dodging German shells and bullets, trying desperately to stay alive on the bloody battlefields of France. He still wore the starched uniform of the US First Infantry Division, the earliest American military unit that saw action in World War I. As far as Billy was concerned, his tenure amounted to one year in hell. He had witnessed firsthand the worst of humanity, and the spectacle had destroyed his innocence and aged him beyond his years. The young man had changed profoundly over the last year; he still bore the appearance of youth, but something in him was badly hurt. It showed in his eyes, in the way he moved and in the nuances of his facial expressions. While he was certain he was keeping his inner scars hidden, his grief was obvious to anyone who had ever known him.

There was one thing that had kept Billy's hope alive while the world burned around him; her name was Julie Sinclair. Throughout his service in the horrific conflict, the young man kept the photograph of his one and only close to his heart. When all looked lost at the Battle of Cantigny, when the air was thick with lead and men were dying all around, Billy pulled out the picture of Julie and stared for long moments at her smiling young face. O'Rielly often swore that a light shone from that small black and white

A heartbroken soldier died in a tragic motorcycle accident, causing a mysterious light to appear near his former home in Ohio.

photo, but it wasn't until the roaring madness at Cantigny, late in May 1918, when he saw a genuine light emanating from the beautiful woman's face, filling him with a sudden and profound calm.

Billy had always loved her, but after Cantigny he became convinced that Julie had saved his life, had kept him sane when everyone and everything around him had slipped into insanity. Every memory he had of her was suddenly cast in a sacred light. For the rest of the war, Billy was lost to dreams of Julie. He escaped from the horror of his surroundings by diving into his memories, where he relived every minute he had spent with his hometown love. He was able to recall everything about her: the musical lilt of her voice, her habit of brushing her hair behind her right ear, how she snorted when struck by a fit of laughter, the way her skin glowed in sun.

He wrote to her religiously, every day, and although he never said as much in his letters, he intended to propose to her upon his return. The idea became nothing less than his reason for living, a vision that he kept alive through the war—even after Julie's letters stopped coming with the same frequency, even after she wrote that it might be best they "remain friends" when he got back home. Billy was far too lovestruck to read between the lines, and the first thing he did after the Germans surrendered was visit a Parisian jeweler, from whom he bought the biggest diamond ring he could afford. Disembarking in New York City, Billy picked up an Indian Motorcycle and hit the road, making his way to Elmore, Ohio, as fast as his bike could carry him.

By the time he exited south off the 105 onto Highway 51, his heart was booming. It struck him then that his murderous past was behind him once and for all. The clear Ohio sky was free of shells, and there wasn't a man alive who had the right to give him a suicidal order. Billy O'Rielly was free, and the love of his life was waiting for him at the end of the road—or so he thought.

Riding through the streets of his hometown, Billy stopped off to pick up some flowers before continuing on to the Sinclair farmhouse, just outside Elmore. He was sweating heavily when he got off his motorbike, suddenly uncomfortable in the thick fabric of his military uniform. His stomach churned in fear and his knees suddenly grew weak. *I'll be damned,* the young man thought to himself, managing a grin. *I may as well be going into battle.*

Resolved to carry out his plan, Billy wiped his palms on his pant legs, remembered the warmth of Julie's smile and made his way to the front porch, clutching the flowers the way a new soldier holds a rifle. He knocked on the door; Mrs. Sinclair answered it.

For a second, she didn't recognize the uniformed man standing in front of her. A moment passed before her face lit up. "Billy!" she cried happily. "You're back!"

"Hello, Mrs. Sinclair," he said to Julie's mother.

"Thank God that you've made it back safely," she said. "We heard such horrible things about Cantigny. Julie was worried sick."

Billy trembled at the sound of Julie's name. It had been so long since he had heard someone else say it. "Thank you, Mrs. Sinclair," he said. "It was a tough thing for sure, but it's over now."

They pair stood on the porch for a few moments, looking at each other awkwardly. Julie's mom stared at the bouquet of flowers Billy held in his hands. Finally, Billy spoke, his heart pounding so hard against his ribcage that it almost hurt. "I was wondering, ma'am, is Julie in?"

Mrs. Sinclair looked down at the porch upon hearing her daughter's name. Billy then knew something was wrong—he hadn't been invited in. He did not know what was going on, but he knew something had changed with

Julie, something he couldn't help. Billy stared helplessly as a dark, heavy cloud passed over him. "I'm sure Julie would love to see you," Mrs. Sinclair responded, trying to remain buoyant. "But she isn't in right now. She's…out."

The soldier reacted almost automatically, stiffly handing the flowers to Mrs. Sinclair. "Thank you, ma'am. Could you give these to Julie please?"

Mrs. Sinclair took the flowers from him. "I will," she said, a heavy trace of sadness now audible in her voice. Billy was halfway down the stairs when Mrs. Sinclair spoke again. "Billy, there's something you should know. Julie…she's engaged."

"Engaged?"

"To Fred McGuire, the butcher's son."

Feeling his legs giving under him, Billy quickened his pace to his motorcycle. "Thank you, ma'am. Please give her my best."

Mrs. Sinclair invited Billy in for some tea, but she spoke too late; her voice was drowned out by the roar of his motorcycle engine. A second later he was gone, tearing off the property. For several minutes Mrs. Sinclair stood at the doorway with the flowers in her hands, watching the trail of dust on her driveway slowly dissipate.

The world suddenly stopped making sense for Billy O'Rielly. For the last year of his life, he had been motivated almost exclusively by his passion for Julie. It had kept hope alive in the horrific face of war, it had calmed him in moments of mortal panic and it had convinced him that Julie was his. A part of him believed he had some sort of psychic contact with Julie Sinclair, which explained why images of her came most vividly when he felt the greatest despair. *She knows I'm in bad,* he would think to himself. *She's here to tell me that it's going to be all right.*

Such ideas seemed a matter of course when he was overseas, but now they were nothing more than desperate palliatives constructed by his own mind to cope with the madness of war. He felt stupid and small. He hit the curve in the road tightly, leaning low into the turn; the Elmore Bridge was just ahead, but Billy couldn't see it. Tears streaked down his expressionless face, casting the world around him into shapeless forms of shadow and color. He was speeding through a surreal landscape of blurred images.

And then he was falling. Billy O'Rielly had been driving blind for about 50 yards when he veered off the road, missing Elmore Bridge and plummeting into the ravine that it spanned. He was killed instantly in the crash, decapitated by a low-hanging branch as he fell to the banks of the Portage River. The irony of his death wasn't lost on any of the locals, who grieved for a young man who had managed to survive one year of war, only to lose his life his first day home.

The dramatic circumstances surrounding Billy O'Rielly's death proved to be fertile ground for gossip, and the unfortunate young soldier quickly became part of Ottawa County's local folklore. His story took on other dimensions over the years, when locals began reporting bizarre sightings on the road to Elmore Bridge—sightings that continue to this very day.

The light was first seen on the evening of March 21, 1920, exactly one year after O'Rielly met his end. A man driving home from town saw a single headlight speeding down toward him. He was halfway across Elmore Bridge

when the approaching motorcycle began to veer dangerously, suddenly swerving to the right edge of the road. It
straightened itself out for only a moment before swerving
off the road altogether. The man in the car yelled out in
surprise, expecting the motorbike to go plummeting over
the edge of the ravine, but it was then that the headlight
suddenly vanished.

The man stopped his car and peered into the bush
alongside Portage River, but nothing stirred underneath.
There was no sound of a crash, no painful cries, no smoking remains of a beat-up motorbike—nothing except the
rushing river beneath him. The man drove home as
quickly as he could. He called the authorities, but after
investigating the site they found no trace of a recent
motorcycle accident, although much of the bush was still
scarred by Billy O'Rielly's lethal mishap exactly one year
before. Coincidences so bizarre are seldom ignored, and
the story of the phantom biker on Elmore Bridge was
born soon after.

If the streaking light just outside of Elmore is indeed
Billy O'Rielly, the years have proven that he must have
been a consistent man while he was alive. For the light
appears without fail every March 21, moving quickly
towards Elmore Bridge before swerving off the road and
vanishing into thin air. Over the years it has been observed
from a number of different angles. Motorists approaching
the bridge from either direction have seen the light head
on or from behind. Those who have stood next to the road
when the light appears say that it is a single ball of light
that vanishes when it reaches the edge of the ravine—there
is neither bike nor rider behind it.

The glow of O'Rielly's headlight is said to appear near the bridge to this very day. It has been the subject of investigation, speculation, exaggeration and local lore. Yet if the light truly is the ghost of Billy O'Rielly reliving the last tortured moments of his life, then the light is essentially a supernatural manifestation of human tragedy. And as fascinating as it might seem, many hope the light will stop appearing one day, and Billy's story will be put to rest.

The Light in Big Thicket

The Bragg Road Light, Big Thicket Light, Ghost Light, Saratoga Light—many names have been given to the recurring supernatural phenomenon that appears among the various flora of the Big Thicket in Hardin County, Texas. The hovering orb of light was first spotted in the 1940s, moving south down Bragg Road after sunset. No one knows for certain how long the light has been there, but it was first observed by human eyes shortly after the railroad between Saratoga and Bragg Station was made into Bragg Road.

The original seven-mile railroad branch was constructed by the Santa Fe Railroad in 1902 to accommodate the oil and logging industries that had suddenly come to life in the county. Oilmen and loggers turned the land into money until the early 1930s, when both oil and lumber had been depleted. By 1934 it was no longer financially feasible to keep the Saratoga track running. The track was pulled up and a county road was laid in its place along the track bed.

The new path was called Bragg Road, and to this day it connects the small town of Saratoga to Farm Road 1293. One of Texas' many scenic backroads, the seven-mile pathway cuts through Big Thicket country, a biologically diverse wilderness that attracts many outdoor enthusiasts. Yet over the years, Bragg Road itself has become something of an attraction. Ever since cars replaced trains along the Big Thicket pathway, motorists have seen the mysterious light, which cast the short road into the canon of Texas folklore.

Although sightings of the Bragg Road Light go back to the 1940s, it was not until 1960 that the phenomenon got statewide attention. In the summer of that year, the now-legendary Texas journalist Archer Fullingim began writing stories about the Bragg Road Light in a Hardin County paper, the Kountz *News.* The stories, featuring different observations and interpretations of the hovering light, were picked up by some of the big publications in Beaumont, Dallas and Houston. What was once a local story suddenly became a curiosity throughout Texas. On weekends, the streets of Saratoga and Kountz filled with cars from all corners of the Lone Star State, packed full of young Texans intent on seeing the Bragg Road Light for themselves. They came on Friday nights, usually with plans to camp for the weekend in the Big Thicket, where they pitched their tents and waited.

As might be imagined, not everyone was a diligent ghost hunter. The road soon became famous for being Hardin County's premier party spot, and those not so interested in ghosts were more than content to spend the weekend quaffing beer and cavorting in the Big Thicket, letting the light serve as an excuse for drunken revelry in the back-woods of Texas. But for individuals eager to collect first-hand evidence of the supernatural, the sojourns to Bragg Road allowed for many transcendental experiences. The light appeared often enough in front of enough witnesses to lend the road a haunted reputation across the nation.

Descriptions of the light are usually quite consistent. Spotted about two hours after sunset, it is a small yellow orb hovering about seven feet above the ground. It always appears about half a mile north of observers, slowly moving south down the road. It grows larger as it comes closer, gradually changing color from yellow to white. As it draws near, it begins to sway from side to side, transforming into a single circle of bright white light. At this point, many observers feel a sudden flush of fear course down their spines. No one has ever really articulated why, but the glowing orb seems to become more frightening than fascinating when it turns white, and more than one trembling spectator has leapt into his vehicle and driven away when it does. Those who remain standing, however, witness the light's color change once more. Drawing even nearer, the harsh white hues of the light acquire amber tinges. By the time it finally comes to a halt about 50 yards away, the stationary light is a dark red, looking almost as if it were observing the observers congregated along the sides of Bragg Road. Then it vanishes.

While the light always behaves similarly, it does not materialize according to any set schedule. The mysterious apparition has been known to light up Bragg Road every night for weeks on end, only to follow up with month-long stretches of absence. Nevertheless, enough people have seen the light to make it one of Texas' most talked-about supernatural phenomena. In October 1974, it was featured in *National Geographic*, and paranormal enthusiasts all across the country have come to Hardin County with hopes of spotting the light.

The theories about the origin of the Bragg Road Light are as numerous as they are fantastical. One tale has the light as the spirit of a 16th-century conquistador who continues to hover over Aztec gold he buried over 400 years ago. Another story, not nearly so wishful, posits that the light is the manifestation of a Texas Jayhawker killed in the Civil War. He was shot during the Kaiser Burnout when Confederate Captain James Kaiser had his soldiers flush out Union sympathizers by setting fire to the bush. If the light is indeed the spirit of a man killed during the Burnout, it wouldn't be the only memento of the Civil War fires that burned in Hardin County. For the Big Thicket still bears scars of the Kaiser Burnout, a stretch where the trees grow thinly and the flora is stunted and sparse.

And then there are the stories of the railroad casualties. One account tells of a train operator decapitated during a train accident late in the 19th century. According to this legend, the light is the dead man's lantern, swinging back and forth as he searches for his missing head along Bragg Road. Or could it be a ghostly manifestation of the souls of Mexican workers who labored on the track? Local folklore has this group of migrant workers falling victim to the murderous parsimony of their foreman. Since he was unwilling to pay the Mexicans for their work, he had them killed just as they hammered the last spike.

There are other explanations for the Bragg Road Light. More scientifically inclined observers speak of the chemical reactions in swamp gases from the Big Thicket or reflections of headlights from cars on Farm Road 1293. Whatever the case, the light continues to attract paranormal enthusiasts from all over the United States. So much so, in fact, that in 1997 Bragg Road was designated Ghost Road Scenic Drive County Park, making the ghost of Bragg Road into one of the small rural county's biggest tourist attractions.

Paulding Light

Robbins Lake Road winds through the woods of Michigan's Upper Peninsula between two quiet northern towns, Paulding and Watersmeet. At the top of a hill about a half-mile west of US 45, you will find a barricade blocking the inconspicuous backroad. There's a sign here put up by the Michigan Forest Service and, on any summer evening, a crowd of observers usually stands around their cars, eagerly scanning the sky for the famous Paulding Light.

The light has been documented by scientists and paranormal experts alike. It elicits all sorts of reactions, from rationally minded theories regarding swamp gas, mineral deposits, reflecting light and electromagnetic energy to supernatural explanations that involve the lingering spirit of a murdered postal worker, a dead railroad brakeman, a broken-hearted engineer and doughty old Pancake Joe.

Although numerous hypotheses abound, it seems that most observers lean towards supernatural conjecture. The

Skeptics and believers alike still flock to Michigan's Upper Peninsula to witness Paulding Light firsthand.

Michigan Forest Service itself endorses the most unscientific of explanations with a placard it erected at the site (see photo).

Yet the ghost of the dead brakeman is only one legend among many. Other storytellers assent that the multicolored glow that dances after dusk is indeed a lantern, but it belongs to a railroad engineer, not a brakeman. This version of bygone mortal strife in Ontonagon County has an engineer confronting a lewd lumberjack in a local pub over rumors the logger was spreading about his one-and-only. The engineer was stabbed in the ensuing fight and died later that night. After he was buried, it became clear that the stories the lumberjack was telling were actually true, that the late engineer's sweetheart was in fact unfaithful. So it is said that the ghost of the engineer still wanders the woods around Paulding, looking for his own soul. In this version, the Paulding Light is the lantern he carries when he goes on his nightly searches.

Another folktale involves one of the state's earliest postal workers, who traded in his horse for a dogsled while working his route during Michigan's snowbound winter months. On a cold January morning, a local hunter's grisly discovery explained why the people in the region had not been getting any letters. There, amid the wreck of a dogsled and scattered mail that had yet to be delivered, lay the corpse of the postman and what was left of his sled team. The bodies of master and dogs alike were frozen in gruesome poses of death. Both were strewn across a stretch of blood-red snow, their throats slit open from ear to ear. The region has been called Dog Meadow ever since, and some people believe that the Paulding Light is the murdered mailman, coming back every night to get his team together.

There is also the story of Pancake Joe, the big man who ran a saloon in Watersmeet and ended up buying a rock farm near Paulding. If it is indeed Pancake Joe's spirit on Robbins Lake Road, it was not a traumatic death but firmly held convictions that caused Joe to linger on after his death. Pancake Joe was a man who shunned civilization and fought the settlement of America's hinterlands to the very end. His temper went bad after power lines went through the area, and he died soon after. This theory has the spirit of Pancake Joe climbing the electric poles and dancing along the lines, sending sparks flying in a tireless attempt to frighten people away from the secluded land that he knew and loved.

Who can say which version of the Paulding Light story is true? Given the variety, probably no one. But come the sub-zero temperatures of the frigid winter or the balmy evenings of Michigan's summer months, the Paulding Light continues to shine, attracting scientific observers, paranormal enthusiasts and undecided onlookers alike.

Ghost Road

The strange lights moving along Mississauga Trail just outside Port Perry, Ontario, make up one of Canada's more famous supernatural accounts. Studied by numerous paranormal investigators and featured on television documentaries, the lights have become something of a local attraction. On any given weekend night in the summer, you can find dozens of cars parked along the side of the road, as spectators wait in clusters of lawn chairs to see a moving ball of light come flying down the road. It is said that on some nights between April and July, the light appears as often as eight times an hour.

Over the years, the light on the road has appeared so consistently that the Mississauga Trail on Scugog Island has been given the unofficial title of "Ghost Road" by Port Perry residents. But the solitary road winding through the woods was not always a supernatural landmark. In fact, it is said that the road was a road just like any other before a gruesome motorcycle accident claimed the life of one man. The facts of the accident, which occurred some time between the 1950s and the 1970s, are sketchy, especially depending upon who's telling the story. Sometimes the man's name is Dan Sweeny, some-times he's Dave Sweeny, but the accounts of his last moments are always the same.

The young man races along Mississauga Trail on a new motorcycle. By all accounts, he was flying down the deserted road with a recklessness reserved for the young. The Mississauga Trail is actually quite short, and it is believed that Sweeny may have overestimated the extent of the paved road. When the road ended suddenly at a farmer's field, he spun out of control and was thrown from his bike. Sweeny was stopped by a barbed wire fence, which caught him around the throat. He was killed instantly.

It is said that the light began appearing on the road not long after the accident took place. Motorists on the Mississauga Trail at night would be startled by a circular white light approaching quickly in their rearview mirrors. Those who swerved out of the way watched as the white light turned into a smaller red light when it passed them. This taillight would suddenly and inexplicably vanish the moment it hit the end of the road. Those who were not able to get out of the light's way in time were terrified that the unidentified vehicle would collide with them. But the light disappeared as quickly as it came, leaving bewildered drivers alone on the suddenly dark road.

These experiences recurred over the years until the people of Port Perry renamed the road where the light appeared. So it was that the Ghost Road was born, and motorists who were on the road late at night became extra wary of a rapidly approaching white light in their rearview mirrors. The mystery of Ghost Road, however,

Passersby gather on a stretch of road in Ontario called the Ghost Road, hoping to see a mysterious, ethereal light.

did not fade once a name was attached to it. Subsequent years brought increasing notoriety, and as people began to gather on the road during summer evenings hoping to spot the phenomenon, alternate explanations for the light on Ghost Road began to circulate.

So many people have been fascinated with the light that many have undertaken their own investigations. Yet not a single person has found any official police document or newspaper report that mentions a motorcycle accident on Scugog Island. Is it shoddy research or simply an instance of an urban legend running amok?

Soon after the story of the dead motorbiker was cast in doubt, another story began to circulate. According to it, the light is the spiritual manifestation of a dead 19th-century farmer. This farmer, embroiled in some feud with his neighbors, was shot in the back while tilling his field. The details of the feud, along with the farmer's name, have faded into the shadows of history. But proponents of this theory believe that the light on Ghost Road is his spirit, which returns nightly to the place the farmer was buried by a large rock that marks the end of the Mississauga Trail. In this version of the story, the focal point isn't the Ghost Road as much as the large rock that lies at the end of the Mississauga Trail. The light moves down the road, disappearing once it reaches the rock. Indeed, there have been other bizarre phenomena associated with this rock. Some who have attempted to sit on it claim to have felt an invisible force throw them quickly off.

Yet in spite of the theories, formal paranormal investigations haven't been able to provide a conclusive explanation for the light's cause. In the meantime, alternate accounts have gained currency. Everything from angry Indian spirits to alien life forms have been offered as possible explanations for the light on Ghost Road.

And then there are the rational theories for the lights. Some state that the lights may be reflections from the headlights of cars on nearby roads. Others note that similar phenomena have been reported all across North America, from Michigan to Texas—flashing, often multicolored lights, repeatedly appearing in certain rural places.

This phenomenon has occurred with such regularity that scientific observers have taken to calling them "Earth Lights," explaining them as either products of chemical reactions from local gases, mineral deposits or some anomalous manifestation of electromagnetic energy.

Despite the official tenor of such scientific jargon, such theories are no more effective in fully explaining the lights than the supernatural stories that inevitably accompany the sightings. So the debate continues. To this day, the white light on Ghost Road is sighted regularly—it remains a kind of open invitation to anyone interested in witnessing a ghost firsthand. Some claim that the casual manner in which the lights on Ghost Road are now treated take away from the mystique of the haunting. Nevertheless, the seemingly sentient light continues to appear, obviously unconcerned with its varying interpretations among the living.

2
Blood on the Road

Some of the most famous highway ghost stories *stem from fatal accidents on the road. The ghosts sometimes appear as they were during their last moments of life, mangled and torn by ugly wounds. And it is these ghosts that tend to interact most with the living, hitching rides with generous motorists, throwing themselves in front of oncoming cars or running motorists off the side of the road in phantom cars of their own. Be warned: the road ahead is slick with blood.*

Resurrection Mary

He swore at the time that she was the most beautiful woman he had ever seen. Her brilliant blonde hair was a sheet of flowing gold cropped just below her shoulders; her eyes, almost impossibly blue, were set in the perfectly shaped oval of her face; and her pale skin, luminescent in the dimly lit hall, looked as smooth as a burnished pearl. She was moving through the crowd at the Willowbrook Ballroom with an inborn grace. Her look of imperturbable calm left the otherworldly beauty of her face undisturbed by a single emotion. She was the aesthetic ideal of a bygone age, the embodiment of a style that women of the silver screen tried to capture years before he was born. But as far as this young man was concerned, Carole Lombard, Greta Garbo or Ingrid Bergman had nothing on the cold splendor of the woman walking towards him. It was unsettling how beautiful she was.

The young man could only stare speechless as the woman approached him. She glided effortlessly through the crowd of revelers at the Willowbrook, not pausing once until she stood right in front of him. Several moments passed before she spoke. "Hello."

The man was just as smitten by the brilliant smile that suddenly spread across the woman's face. He smiled back. "Hello."

Another moment or two passed before she spoke again. "Would you care to dance?"

The man would never be able to remember how he responded to this question, but he spent the rest of the night on the ballroom dance floor, spinning through every number the band performed in a hypnotic state. As far as he was concerned, it was only the two of them, dancing close as one song blended into another. While some words passed between them, the next morning he could not remember what they were. Nor would he be able to remember when exactly they left or how they made their way to his car. But he was able to recall a feeling of inevitability, almost of helplessness; he was in full knowledge that this strange woman was directing the course of the evening, that he had absolutely no say in what was happening. It was all he could do to look at her and remember who he was himself.

They were soon driving down Archer Avenue towards an uncertain destination. The man knew he was taking the woman home, but he wasn't sure where home was. He knew he was supposed to be driving down Archer, but he wasn't sure how he knew—in fact, he wasn't sure if she had said a word since she had gotten in his car. Yet somehow he knew he was taking her where she wanted to go.

The surreal encounter concluded quite suddenly when they passed Resurrection Cemetery. The young man felt suddenly alert, as if he had just snapped out of a strange dream. Looking over to the passenger side, he stared in amazement at the empty seat next to him. Outside, the countless tombstones of Resurrection Cemetery were barely visible, rushing by just beyond the glow of the streetlights.

So ended another encounter with Resurrection Mary, one of Chicago's most famous ghosts. Haunting the suburb of Justice since the early 1930s, beautiful and unsettling Resurrection Mary has enthralled, bewitched and horrified hundreds of Chicagoans. Her origins are tragically similar to so many spirits that come back to haunt the places they knew when they were alive. She was a young woman, taken before her time, killed in a freak accident along Archer Avenue late one winter night in 1934.

According to local legend, her name was Mary Bregavy, a youthful Polish immigrant of remarkable beauty, who could make hearts race and palms sweat with a single glance. Although she spoke very little, her charm made her one of Justice's most popular people, and she spent most of her weekends at the old O'Henry Ballroom (the Willowbrook today) with her beau, dancing into the small hours of the evening.

Things went sour one evening at the O'Henry when Mary's boyfriend grew resentful at all the attention she was getting from other men. Taking her aside, he began berating her for what he perceived as playful reciprocation. Mary did not respond well to her boyfriend's accusations and, tearing herself from his covetous grasp, made her way out of the crowded ballroom and into the cold January night. Whether her boyfriend's jealous eyes detected genuine flirtation or not would be reduced to a forgettable detail in Mary's legend.

The wind was cold and fierce as Mary strode away from the ballroom. Snow began falling when she reached Archer Avenue, and before long she was staggering through a raging blizzard. Mary had left the ballroom in such haste that she didn't bother to take her coat with her—an oversight she regretted as she tried to make her way down the nearly deserted, snow-choked street. She began to grow desperately cold when a pair of headlights appeared from out of the night behind her. Hoping to get a ride in the approaching automobile, Mary leapt onto the road, waving her arms to get the driver's attention. It would be her last conscious action.

The driver was navigating through the thick snowfall with more than a little difficulty. Knowing he wouldn't be able to make any abrupt stops, he relied on his familiarity with the road to keep him out of any trouble. So he knew there was going to be trouble when Mary suddenly appeared in his headlights, no more than a dozen yards ahead. He slammed on the breaks violently, but it was too late. Skidding out of control, the driver saw the look of terror on Mary's face just before he plowed into her.

The car skid a few more yards before finally coming to a stop. Although barely able to discern the figure lying on the ground in his rearview mirror, the driver could make out enough to see that wide crimson streaks were spreading across the white of her dress and the snow she lay upon. Dumbstruck by the violence of the collision, he only sat there staring for a few minutes before the horrible realization of what happened dawned on him. Reacting more out of fear than anything else, he stepped on the gas and sped out into the stormy night, leaving the dead body of Mary Bregavy on the road. The snow gathered over her open eyes and melted in the blood-soaked fabric of her elegant white dress.

The identity of the driver was never discovered, and Mary was buried shortly after in nearby Resurrection Cemetery. Yet while her life was effectively terminated on that dark January night, Mary's story had just begun. Accounts of strange experiences on Archer Avenue began about five years later. Drivers on the road at night told of their run-ins with a disturbingly beautiful woman in a white dress. During the winter months, a blonde-haired woman would suddenly appear on the side of the road, waving for assistance.

Because Mary's dress seems inadequate for the frigid evening temperature, motorists almost always stop to let her in. Throughout the years, she has invariably been described as extraordinarily attractive, with cold blue eyes and brilliant blonde hair, dressed in a thin white dress. Many have commented on the notable lack of animation in her voice when she asks for a lift, while others, so taken with her ethereal beauty, have not been able to recall what she says, let alone how she sounds when she says it. But all remember driving north on Archer Avenue with this stunning woman on the passenger side, waiting for further directions on where to let her off. They never seem to drive beyond Resurrection Cemetery. For the moment they pass by the front gates of the sprawling cemetery, the mysterious woman suddenly vanishes.

Others have witnessed different manifestations of the active spirit on Archer Avenue. Some motorists have been shocked out of the peaceful stillness of their nocturnal commutes at the sight of a woman's disembodied head hovering by the side of the road. It is seen floating just outside Resurrection Cemetery, looking blankly at terrified drivers going by. She matches the description of the hitchhiker on Archer Avenue, with blonde hair, blue eyes and incredible beauty. Her head never remains for long, disappearing in the moment it takes for drivers to glance over their shoulders.

As startling as such sightings have been, the pale apparition has also been responsible for more than one near-car accident over the years. No one knows why she seems to grow so animated at times, but more than once she has been known to run at cars as they pass by the entrance to Resurrection Cemetery, approaching terrified motorists with a preternatural speed. She has even jumped up on the sides of some vehicles, standing on the sideboards of moving cars as frightened drivers swerve on the road, trying to recover from their sudden terror. In the next instant she is gone, leaving stunned motorists wondering if they might be going mad.

Yet as these events continued to occur over the years, locals began to accept the presence of the ghost near Resurrection Cemetery. Fright-filled accounts were recounted across the state. Before long, people connected the beautiful phantom to the death of Mary Bregavy in 1934. The physical characteristics of the ghost loosely matched the descriptions people offered of the young Polish woman while she was alive, except, perhaps, for a strange hypnotic quality she never displayed. The specter's attachment to Resurrection Cemetery—the same graveyard where Mary Bregavy was buried—was not lost on locals, and the phantom of Archer Avenue was soon named Resurrection Mary. Her unusually frequent appearances among Chicagoans would make her one of America's most famous spirits.

Resurrection Mary does not seem to mind the attention. As the years have passed, incidents on Archer Avenue have ensured that her legend remains current. Even today, cab drivers driving at night are extra cautious while driving down the now-infamous stretch of road, all too mindful of the stories of a woman in white suddenly appearing in front of motorists. Every one of them knows someone who knows someone who, in a moment of incredible fear, has run over the young pedestrian, only to see her vanish the moment she comes into contact with the car hood. Ever-increasing numbers of young men claim to have spent strange, almost dream-like evenings with a mysterious woman they met in the Willowbrook. Their stories are always the same. They spend the whole night dancing with the young woman, after which she asks them for a ride home. She gives directions that lead north up Archer Avenue, but no man has ever found out where her home is, for without fail she always vanishes when they pass the gate outside Resurrection Cemetery.

Perhaps the cemetery is Mary's new home. If this indeed is the case, there is some evidence that she isn't happy about it. The most famous sighting of the young ghost occurred one night in December 1977 when a passing motorist noticed the lightly dressed apparition just inside the cemetery. She was standing against the bronze barrier of the front gate, her bone-white hands clenched around two bars, pulling at them desperately. She looked distressed and angry as she yanked on the cemetery gate.

The man stopped at a nearby payphone to call the police, reporting that a young woman was trapped in Resurrection Cemetery. By the time the authorities arrived, she was gone. This isn't to say that there was no trace of the woman in question. For two of the bronze bars were inexplicably damaged. Both were warped and bent, as if they had been transformed by some immense heat. If this discovery wasn't strange enough, the police noticed that two handprints were pressed into both of the damaged bars—evidence of the strength of some unusually powerful being. When word of the damage at the cemetery gates spread throughout the community, the spirit of Resurrection Mary became the accepted explanation. Soon afterwards, people were coming from near and far to look at the ghostly handprints embedded in the warped metal.

Embarrassed by the public furor over the damaged gate, the cemetery authorities tried to provide alternate explanations. They spread word about a loading truck that had backed up into the gate. When people brought up the handprints in the bent bars, officials changed their story, claiming that steelworkers had accidentally damaged the gate while working on it; the marks on the gate were caused by their hands, encased in protective welders' gloves. No one thought much of this explanation, and as crowds continued to congregate around the graveyard gates, the staff at Resurrection Cemetery decided to take drastic measures. A week before Halloween in 1978, the two troublesome bars were removed completely, effectively putting an end to the controversy.

Although the physical evidence may have been removed from public sight, nothing could erase the warped bars from the public memory. After the incident at the gates, Resurrection Mary became something of a supernatural celebrity. To this day, her name is synonymous with the "vanishing hitchhiker" story that is told and retold across the country. Many people describing their experiences with phantom commuters on American roadsides will often talk of their own "Resurrection Mary–type" encounters with similar details.

In fact, the Resurrection Mary story has achieved the greatest prominence among highway hauntings. Perhaps this honor reflects her striking looks or the tragedy of her death. Or perhaps her fame might be attributed to the frequency of her appearances along Archer Avenue and in the Willowbrook Ballroom. Whatever the case, the legend of Resurrection Mary continues today. Young men in the Willowbrook still report their mesmerizing encounters with an astonishing young beauty, while motorists driving Archer Avenue late at night continue to spot the well-dressed specter on the side of the road, waiting for a ride home to the desolate rows of tombstones in Resurrection Cemetery.

Hot Rod Haven

Mitchell Hill Road winds through the wooded hills of Jefferson County just south of Louisville, Kentucky. Apart from its abrupt twists and hairpin turns, little about the road would strike a motorist as odd during daylight hours. But come sunset, everything about Mitchell Hill Road changes. Surrounding greenery is transformed into twisted limbs that seem to clutch at passing vehicles when the moon rises. Where in daylight the forest teems with sylvan life, at night something intangible and sinister glares out from the darkened woods. Many of those driving on Mitchell Hill Road in the evening have claimed that even the road itself portends doom. The pavement

A illegal racing strip known for fatal crashes, "Hot Rod Haven" in Kentucky remains a hub of paranormal activity.

rolling under their cars' tires seems to announce certain death waiting around the very next bend.

For far too many motorists, Mitchell Hill Road's menacing promise has not been an empty one. From the 1940s to the 1970s, groups of young Kentuckians all over Jefferson County gathered atop Mitchell Hill on weekend evenings, bent on making mischief along the road that bears the hill's namesake. They were mostly adolescent males willing to risk death and affluent enough to have the vehicles that might take them there. They raced down the side of the street in pairs, selecting Mitchell Hill Road because it was the most treacherous route they could find, with enough straightaways to allow racers to gather up enough steam and sudden corners tight enough to be lethal. Every generation brought the best cars of their day to race against one another, and Mitchell Hill Road was eventually renamed Hot Rod Haven for all the sleek vehicles flying down it on Friday and Saturday nights. They raced roadsters in the 50s and muscle cars in the 70s; meanwhile, the body count on the treacherous stretch of road mounted.

Disasters were inevitable. Boys taking the straights too fast and the turns too wide found themselves flying off the road and crashing through the bush; many of these accidents resulted in only cuts or bruises, broken windshields and deformed bumpers, but every now and again, the crashes were horrific. Legend has it that more than 25 people were killed in the 40 years that the road was used as a racetrack. Rescue workers pulled more than enough bodies out of smoking ruins off the side of Mitchell Hill Road to turn the winding path into the region's most lethal stretch of road.

Hot Rod Haven came to occupy a dark place in the public consciousness. By the 1970s, Mitchell Hill Road was treated with the same gravity as a tomb. Although no one thought much of the cemetery atop Mitchell Hill in the 1940s, 40 years later it was deemed morbidly appropriate that Hot Rod Haven ran by a graveyard.

It was appropriate because many people believed that Mitchell Hill Road was heavy with supernatural traffic. No one knows who spotted the phantom car first, but in the late 1960s a sleek roadster began appearing on the straightaway at night. The car was said to be a slightly luminescent white, vaguely transparent, with the darkened woods slightly visible behind it. While no one could clearly make out the driver, it was apparent that someone was indeed behind the wheel.

Whoever the driver was, he had no concern for anyone else on the road. Some motorists have veered out of their lanes to avoid colliding with the oncoming roadster, while others, too slow to react, are only able to gape into the rearview mirror as the car passes straight through them. Always appearing on the longest straightaway on Mitchell Hill, the shimmering vehicle is traveling at top speed when it hits the sharp left turn in the road. Horrified drivers who have witnessed the spectacle stare helplessly as the roadster spins out of control and goes flying off the road. But the violent collision that should take place never occurs, for the car suddenly vanishes into thin air just before crashing into the surrounding trees.

This phantom roadster is still spotted regularly by motorists traveling Mitchell Hill Road by night, but it isn't the only one. Indeed, since the ghostly vintage sports car made its first appearance about 40 years ago, numerous other makes and models have been spotted swerving along Hot Rod Haven before vanishing into thin air. Souped-up GTOs, Chevy Novas, Dodge Chargers, Ford Mustangs, Corvette Stingrays and Pontiac Trans-Ams —supernatural versions of all these cars have been seen racing down the side of Mitchell Hill, disappearing the moment they fly off the road.

So keep your eyes open if you are traveling along Mitchell Hill Road at night. If a shimmering white vehicle should suddenly appear in the rearview mirror, don't panic—it's just one of the ghosts of Hot Rod Haven. But be sure to keep your eyes on the road and your speed down. The last thing Jefferson County needs is another ghost on Mitchell Hill.

The Legend of the Dead Prom Date

The legend of the young ghost on Arkansas' Highway 365 begins on a rainy June evening sometime in the 1950s. A single vehicle races south on the narrow road a few miles south of Little Rock, its headlights cutting through the wind and the rain as it rushes to its destination. It is a stormy night, and the landscape is brought to life by violent forces of nature. Lightning streaks across a menacing sky, periodically lighting up the windswept chaos of the wild night.

The big old Chevy speeds through the storm, seemingly oblivious to the natural bedlam occurring all around. And indeed, for the two teenagers inside the car, the terrible show on the other side of the windshield is just that—a show, a dramatic backdrop for the exciting evening that lies ahead. It's prom night, and the young couple sitting in the car are far too preoccupied with the idea of the upcoming celebration to give the storm too much attention. They are dressed to the nines, bright-eyed and exuberant about the end of school, singing along with Elvis Presley as he croons "All Shook Up" through the car radio.

Everything changes in the time it takes for a bolt of lightning to streak from the cloudy heavens to the water-logged ground below. The car's tires slide on the wet pavement and the car spins out of control. The girl only gets a chance to let out a scream before the vehicle careens off the road, flying into the ditch and flipping over as the sudden plunge into the deep roadside furrow sends the trunk catapulting over the hood. The car rolls through two full flips, hood over trunk, before it is brought to an abrupt stop by a broad tree lying a dozen or so yards off the highway. The vehicle crashes into the trunk with a horrendous crunch, transformed into little more than a heap of crumpled metal and smoking machinery.

As for the two teenagers in the car, the boy is twisted over the steering wheel, the top half of his body lying over the hood on the wrong side of a smashed windshield. He is dead. The girl is still alive. She is barely holding onto consciousness, trying to focus through a thick fog of mortal shock. Somehow managing to open the passenger door, she stumbles out of the car and into the downpour. Badly bruised and bleeding heavily, the young girl lurches toward the highway. She is just able to make it to the road before she collapses unconscious on the narrow shoulder. By the time a passing car screeches to a halt in front of the prostrate prom date, she too has given up the ghost.

The stretch of highway between Woodson and Redfield has never been the same since. Over they years, countless motorists driving over the Pulaski County line at night have caught sight of a white humanoid shape hovering on the peripheries of their headlights. She comes into focus for a split second—a badly hurt young woman, dressed in a tattered and bloodstained white dress—before vanishing into the darkness of the roadside. Those who do stop and back up to where they spotted the girl are only greeted by the black night and a chorus of frogs and crickets.

For others, the encounter with this young woman has been a more harrowing experience. These motorists, who stop at the sight of the girl in the ruined white dress to find her still standing there, have gotten closer to the legend of Highway 365 than they ever might wish. It is a mystery why she picks some cars and not others, but those who are chosen to give her a ride back to Woodson are never the same.

She is always described as deathly pale, the color of her skin almost matching the hue of her dress, which would be rather elegant if not for the numerous rips and bloodstains across the fabric. Her disheveled blonde hair falls chaotically around her shoulders, partially concealing a black eye underneath. Yet everyone who has been treated to a close look at the girl and the wounds that claimed her so many years ago has stated that she is eerily calm, somehow oblivious to her ugly bruises and deep gashes.

Whether drivers react with noisy urgency or shocked reticence, the gravely wounded young woman always responds with the same vacant tone. With a completely emotionless expression on her face, she asks, "Can you please drive me back to Woodson? I have to get back home." Some have noted that her lips barely move as she speaks these words, yet her voice is imbued with an unnatural gravity, which rings loudly against the heavy silence that descends over the area the moment she begins to talk. Her voice echoes in the small confines of the car when she gives the address; some have claimed that they were hearing a voice from a great distance or at the other end of a long tunnel.

The short drive back to Woodson is always an uncomfortably quiet trip. Any questions asked of the girl fail to elicit a response. She has always sat impassively in the same stony silence, unable or unwilling to answer her drivers' queries. Many of those who have picked up the distressed girl claim that the ride into Woodson seemed to last forever, although it's only a few miles into town from the county line. The entire time, the young girl sits in an incomprehensible silence, staring ahead blankly without betraying a single emotion.

The uneasy silence is broken when driver and passenger arrive at their destination. Pulling up in front of the Woodson home, many motorists claim to hear the girl speak in the same hollow voice. "Thank you, I have to go now." Others don't hear a thing; they do the talking instead, informing their passenger they've arrived. All report feeling their stomachs flutter before finding the girl's seat suddenly vacant. There is no sign that she was ever there or that the car door was ever opened.

Those motorists who are convinced their passenger was not a hallucination have gotten out of their cars to talk to the residents of the house. The first few inquisitive individuals to give the phantom hitchhiker a ride were greeted with hysterical responses. Two tearful parents would explain that their daughter had died during a horrible car accident on her prom night.

As the years passed, however, the parents got used to the nightly visitors coming in with the same grave inquiries about the girl who just directed them to their house. Every year, the frequency of these unwanted visitors increased around June, the same month their daughter died in the car accident. And even after the parents moved out and passed on, the visitations continued. It seems that the ghostly hitchhiker is unaware of the passage of time, still intent on returning home to a mother and father who are long gone.

So it is that all subsequent inhabitants of the house in Woodson have been treated to nocturnal visits from confused drivers who have just had an encounter with the ghost of Highway 365. As for the ghost herself, the young woman has spooked her way into the local folklore. The lonely spirit has become Polaski County's very own vanishing hitchhiker, who, to this very day, continues to scare motorists driving through central Arkansas on hot summer nights.

Highway 666

Highway 666 is probably the most infamous stretch of asphalt in the United States. It consists of roughly 200 miles of road running from the town of Monticello, Utah, to Gallup, New Mexico, and cuts through southwestern Colorado along the way. The highway bisects some of the starkest yet awe-inspiring country in North America. It is a world of rock, shrub, cactus and dirt where the days are hot and dry and the nights are ominously alive with a force that few can articulate. People are few and far between in this part of the country; the small towns along the highway seem to stand in a sort of desperate opposition to the enormous environs. Acting as a lifeline, the lone highway reaches out into the desolate horizon, marked every half an hour or so with ominous, wind-beaten road signs: a white shield on a black background, stamped with the menacing digits 666.

It is here that John the Evangelist's biblical prophecies meet the numbering plan developed by the United States' Joint Board on Interstate Highways. Whereas John declares "666" to be the "number of the beast" in the Book of Revelations, the highway authorities state that the route acquired its number through a purely objective numbering system. In other words, systematic classification, not devilish machination, gave this lonesome road its controversial name.

And yet all the horrific tales that surround this single highway seem to affirm the opposite. The years have seen countless terrors and atrocities heaped along Highway 666. Not only have an inordinate number of fatalities occurred in traffic accidents along the desert road, but many motorists driving the highway have witnessed phenomena that have changed their perspectives forever.

According to the folklore, Highway 666 is a road of the dead. The number of unidentified corpses found along the shoulder over the years would be proof enough for such a claim, but the evidence is even more compelling. For the same force that draws killers to dump their victims along the side of this highway seems to manifest itself in a number of horrifying embodiments: visions of fear and evil that are frequently reported on the thoroughfare, causing more than one road trip to be suddenly rescheduled—if not ended altogether.

Such was the case for "Jordan Ashley," a Salt Lake City native who uses a pseudonym when relating his experiences on Highway 666. "I was driving back home after a business trip to Albuquerque, and took the Highway 666 exit off the I40 at Gallup. The sun was just starting to go down when I hit the 666. I've done a lot of driving through New Mexico, so I knew all about the stories. They're everywhere. 'Don't drive the 666 at night,' they say. 'It's Satan's Speedway or the Highway to Hell.' Of course, they say the worst thing you can do is drive the road when there's a full moon out. But at the time, I wasn't much of a believer, and didn't really think twice at the sight of this big fat orange moon coming up on the horizon."

Ashley wouldn't have paid attention to the moon at all if there hadn't been such a spectacular sunset. "Growing up in Utah, I've seen some pretty amazing skies at the end of the day, but I'd never seen anything like this before. I mean, these red clouds came out of nowhere, looked like

Haunted highway or hoax? Some eyewitnesses claim that their unsettling experiences on Highway 666 are no coincidence.

they were ink that was spilled across the sky. And when I say they were red, they were really, really red. It looked like the sky was bleeding."

He hadn't been on Highway 666 long when a sudden fear began to creep over him. To this day, Ashley has difficulty articulating the sensation. "I don't know how to describe it," he says, "but it had something to do with this real strong feeling that I didn't belong on the road. Like the sun was taking forever to set and there was this incredible red light all around, and just the sight of the sky was starting to freak me out. And it wasn't just the sky; the whole desert turned red, everything was different shades of the same color. My stomach started to get really tight, and right then I just wanted to get out of there as soon as I could."

The problem was that there was nowhere to go but forward. The highway stretched all the way out to the horizon, where it was nothing but more of the same. Ashley entered the enormous Navajo Indian Reservation in the northwestern corner of New Mexico shortly after 9:30 PM. He had been driving through the reservation for about another half hour when the sun finally sank beneath the horizon, blanketing the desert in a silvery darkness. That's when the car appeared in his rearview mirror—two headlights in the distance, quite a distance behind.

"I got a lump in my throat the moment I saw those lights in my mirror. There's no reason to get scared of a car coming up behind you," Ashley says, laughing in spite of himself. "And believe me, I don't normally scare easily, but the sight of this guy's lights put the fear of God in me. I knew then that this situation was no good. A part of me was tempted to turn around and get off the 666, but that would mean driving towards whoever was coming up behind."

Ashley decided his best option was to cover the rest of the highway as quickly as possible. He vowed to never take the 666 again and put his foot down, hoping to make it to Monticello within the next hour and a half. Flying across the desert at over 80 miles per hour, he didn't mind in the least that the car behind him would soon be out of sight. Or so he thought.

"I couldn't believe it," Ashley says today. "I was pushing close to 90 miles an hour in the dark and the car behind me was still getting closer. And he was getting closer fast. I know it seems totally impossible, but this car must've been going well over 100 miles an hour. The lights kept getting bigger and bigger in my rearview mirror, until the car was about 50 yards behind me. That's when he put his brights on, and the inside of my car lit up like it was daytime."

Ashley began panicking, swerving into the other lane in an attempt to get the car off his back, but the car imitated his every move. A second later, the car was riding his bumper, and Ashley, now desperate, drove his car off the road. Skidding out of control as his tires hit the desert, he looked out at the vehicle as it roared past on the highway. He couldn't believe what he saw. "There was no way a car that big could be going that fast. I couldn't see too clearly in the dark, but I was able to make out that it was a big black sedan…an older car too. Like maybe an early 70s Ford Galaxie or something. It was a boat. What's more, it looked like the car might have been overheating; there was smoke streaming out from under its hood and off the roof. The smoke looked silver in the moonlight."

But Ashley wasn't able to gawk at the automobile for long. He was plowing over sand and rock off-road, going far too fast for comfort. He tried to get back on the highway but spun out of control when one of his tires went out on him. By this time, Ashley was convinced that his car was going to roll and grimaced in terrified silence, waiting for the worst. He was lucky; the car made a few more wild revolutions before it skidded to a halt in the dirt.

Somehow the terrified man was thinking with amazing clarity. "When the car finally stopped, I didn't slow down for a second. I got out, threw open the trunk and went to work. There was this urgency. I didn't want to be stationary for any longer than I had to. It felt like I was in hostile territory."

It wasn't long before this feeling was confirmed. "I'd almost finished putting the spare on when the air was filled with the sound of howling. It sounded like they were everywhere, a pack of roving dogs, and although I couldn't see them I knew beyond a shadow of a doubt that they were coming for me."

He left his torn tire lying in the dirt, jumped into his car and roared back onto the road, leaving a cloud of dust behind him. Just as he began to pick up speed on the 666 he spotted what he swore was over a dozen enormous dogs loping along the road behind him. Their eyes shone yellow in the night. Ashley drove the rest of Highway 666 as fast as his car could take him, reaching Monticello within the hour. As might be imagined, he has strong feelings about Highway 666 today. "I will never drive that highway again; no one could pay me enough to spend 20 minutes on that road."

Although Ashley's experience on Highway 666 was terrifying, it doesn't compare to some of the other stories about the highway. Ghost lore runs thick over the road; opinions vary on where fact ends and fiction begins in these innumerable accounts, but almost every paranormal enthusiast who has studied Highway 666 agrees that there is considerable supernatural activity there.

The different phantoms that are said to haunt the road are as varied as they are malicious. A good many motorists have had experiences similar to Ashley's, being run off the road by a black automobile that roars past at an impossible speed (the car is dubbed "Satan's Sedan"). Sometimes this vehicle doesn't run drivers down, but comes at them head on, playing chicken with terrified commuters who inevitably pull off the road to avoid the maniac in the smoking black vehicle. Some have speculated that many of the accidents that occur on the 666 may be a result of the high-speed showdowns with the suicidal driver in the mysterious car.

Then there are the stories of the hounds. Described as a pack of vicious dogs that are able to chase down cars at amazing speeds, these animals have been called Highway 666's "Hounds of Hell." They are capable of shredding car tires with their teeth and leaping through the windows of moving vehicles to maul hapless commuters while they are driving. According to Jordan Ashley's account, a pack of dogs set upon him while he was putting his spare back on. Could these have been the very same Hounds of Hell that have reportedly been responsible for the demise of so many?

Those hapless individuals who have been stranded on Highway 666 are said to be vulnerable to another malevolent vehicle that is known to travel up and down the road. This vehicle is an enormous rig colored a deep crimson and is believed to be piloted by a soulless trucker who has a virulent hatred for any living thing on the side of the road. It is said that this rig moves at a phenomenal speed, plowing into anyone who happens to be standing on the shoulder. Legend has it that dozens of hitchhikers have met their end on the steaming grill of this massive semi.

With such a wide array of malevolent spirits on this single stretch of highway, the apparition of the pale young girl in the white nightgown seems strangely out of place.

Of all the ghostly legends on Highway 666, she is the only one that has been observed during daylight and evening hours. Encounters with this young girl have always been described as eerie experiences, but she had never caused anyone any harm.

She always appears on the shoulder of the highway, looking oddly out of place in the dirty landscape. The sickly pallor of her skin contrasts sharply with her long black hair and disturbingly large eyes, which stare unblinking at oncoming motorists. She stands barefoot in the desert, her white nightgown hanging from her narrow shoulders. So sad is her silent expression that almost every driver who sees her is induced to pull over. Yet she never sticks around long enough to answer people's concerned queries, usually vanishing into the hot desert air before most individuals have finished asking her where her parents are. Who this girl is, and what her spirit is doing in a place so full of hostile paranormal phenomena, remains unclear.

The story behind Highway 666 is also a mystery. It is doubtful that the Joint Board of Interstate Highways created a road saturated with malevolent energy simply by attaching the wrong numbers to it. Do the three sixes form such a potent force that they are able to curse any object they are attached to? Have the "666" signposts along the highway cursed it for good? Some have speculated that the highway runs through sacred Navajo lands, causing ancient Indian spirits, angry at being forgotten by modern America, to unleash their fury on drivers. In any event, drivers are advised to avoid Highway 666—especially if it is nighttime and a full moon is rising over the desert.

Accident on Blue Bell Hill

Strange things have been afoot on Blue Bell Hill for years now. The hill marks the high point of a chalk bluff that rises from the southeast corner of England, about four miles north of the town of Maidstone in the county of Kent. Dominated by busy highway A229, Blue Bell Hill is one of those "neither here nor there" locations, defined more by the near-constant stream of north-south traffic on the A229 than anything else. Indeed, if it weren't for the bizarre happenings that have been occurring on the spot since the late 1960s, next to no one would notice that Blue Bell Hill was even there. But as the stomping grounds for two of England's most prevalent roadside ghosts, Blue Bell Hill has become something of an international attraction.

One of the apparitions is a young woman who appears near the Aylesford turn-off on the southbound side of the road. Seen by dozens of people since the early 1970s, she is usually described as an attractive woman with dark hair and big eyes, clad in a sprawling white dress and no older than 25 years old. Sightings of the young woman wouldn't be so horrifying if they didn't all end in the same traumatic way. For every person who has seen the woman on the A229 has ended up noticing her far too late, frantically pounding on the brakes before plowing into her.

Different drivers have leapt out of their cars cursing, weeping or silently festering in frantic anxiety. Was she dead? Were they to blame? Who was she? Why was this well-dressed woman walking along the highway? Before anyone can answer these questions, she vanishes. There isn't a trace of her. No blood, no dents in the car, not a shred of her big white dress, not a thing. Some have doubted their senses, others have doubted their sanity, but as the number of sightings of the woman on Blue Bell Hill increased, people began to accept that the A229 was haunted.

It wasn't long before a theory about the origin of the haunting emerged. The tragic story dates back to the evening of November 19, 1965. Four women from the town of Gillingham were on a tear; one of them was a bride-to-be who was to be married the next day. She was decked out in her bridal dress, celebrating her last night of freedom with her bridal party. They were flying over Blue Bell Hill in a Mark 1 Ford Cortina when disaster struck. A Jaguar approaching on the other side of the road swerved into their lane just before they were about to pass.

In all the time it takes to gasp, death's scythe swept through the Mark 1, killing three of the passengers in the car, including the future bride. The driver in the Jaguar walked away unharmed. The accident garnered a great deal of press throughout Kent, and for a short time the public mourned along with the friends, relatives and fiancé of the deceased. Such a tragedy, in which the bride and two of her bridesmaids are killed only hours before the wedding, is not easily forgotten. And so when the dark-haired apparition began appearing on the A229 soon afterwards, everyone's thoughts went back to the brutal November 19 accident.

The first collision with the spectral jaywalker is believed to have taken place in the fall of 1966, roughly a year after the fatal accident. An anonymous phone call came into the

Maidstone police station switchboard late at night. The man on the line was obviously distressed, mumbling about a girl that he had run into on Blue Bell Hill. When the switchboard operator asked where he was and what the girl's condition was, the man's voice rose to a frantic pitch. "I bleedin' know where I am!" he yelled into the telephone. "As for the girl, your guess is as good as mine!"

With these words, the panicked man hung up, leaving local authorities wondering about the call. Two officers were sent to investigate Blue Bell Hill, but they couldn't find any trace of an accident. It would be the first of many puzzling reports to the Maidstone police about the disappearing girl in the white dress. For a few years during the early 1970s, these frightened reports were made so regularly that the local authorities began dismissing them. "What you saw, sir," the dispatcher would say to a concerned motorist, "was the ghost of Blue Bell Hill. She was killed the night before her wedding day quite some time ago. Apparently, she's still a bit miffed about it."

Many believed that the unfortunate woman's spirit might find some peace after the thoroughfare she was killed on was replaced by the A229, which was completed in 1972. But it appears she's been more than willing to confront the increased traffic on the new, well-lit highway. If anything, the harrowing encounters with the woman in white have increased since the A229 was constructed, reaching a peak in the early 1990s.

Around the same time another apparition began to appear in the area. Most of the reports came from the dark Old Chatham Road a few miles west of the A229. The encounters with this mysterious spirit, also once a

woman, were far more sinister than the repeated colli-
sions with the ghost on the highway. This woman was not
young, but old; not pretty, but freakishly hideous. She
instills nothing but terror into those unfortunate drivers
who have passed by her.

In his book, *The Ghost of Blue Bell Hill and Other Road
Ghosts,* Sean Tudor reports what is believed to be the first
encounter with this specter. It happened late in the
evening on January 6, 1993. The Maiden family was
returning home to Rochester in a car packed full with one
driver and four passengers. Angela Maiden's daughter was
fast asleep, but everyone else was wide awake when the car
rounded the large bend about 300 yards north of the
Lower Bell crossroads. The Old Chatham Road, hemmed
in by heavy bush, isn't flanked by a single streetlight, and
Mr. Maiden made his way down the road slowly, his visi-
bility limited to his vehicle's bright beams.

No one could blame him for over-reacting when he saw
the dim image of the elderly woman on the road in front of
him. Mr. Maiden instantly slowed down. "What in blazes is
that woman doing out here at this hour?" he exclaimed.

As the family drew closer to the strange pedestrian,
they could make her out in greater detail. She looked to be
quite advanced in years, hunched over as she took small
steps from the right side of the road to the left. It wasn't
until they got even closer to her that they began to feel a
strange foreboding. There was something about her that
wasn't right. She wore an antiquated bonnet and clutched
a torn and tattered shawl around her shoulders. Everyone
in the car was drawn to her right hand, her only visible
body part, which held her shawl together. Illuminated by

the headlights, the skin of her hand seemed impossibly white, and her fingernails were grotesquely long, giving the appendage an eerie claw-like quality. Her dress resembled those that appear in period movies and was a little bit too long, dragging behind her as she made her way across the street.

Mr. Maiden initially intended to ask the woman if she needed any help. He slowed down to a near stop, but was suddenly unsure. Everyone in the car was quiet, wrestling with inexplicable fear of the figure before them. When the woman turned her head to face them, each person in the car was overcome by a sudden gut-wrenching terror. Her eyes were small and black as ink, like pinpoints of malevolent energy that conveyed an utter hatred for everyone in the car. Acting on pure adrenaline, Mr. Maiden put his foot down hard just as the woman opened her mouth wide and lifted a handful of twigs high in her left hand. In the next instant, the car was filled with a hissing noise, even though the car windows were rolled up and the old woman was rapidly receding behind them. Thus went the first encounter with the witch of Old Chatham Road.

Since that January evening, accounts of the sinister hag were reported throughout the year, occurring with the greatest frequency in the winter months, from late November to early February. Who she is and why she has only begun to appear over the last decade is anyone's guess.

It has been suggested that Kent's history of human settlement provides a strong basis for supernatural activity. Tombs and mysterious stone formations dating to prehistoric times have been found across the countryside of southeastern England. It is a popular local theory that countless ancient graves were probably dug up and defaced over the course of modern settlement.

Could it be that the spirits of the United Kingdom's first peoples are responsible for the bizarre goings-on over Blue Bell Hill? Is it the power of their discontented souls that brings the unfortunate bride back to the spot where she was killed, to relive her death over and over again? Do they have something to do with the horrible apparition that currently stalks Old Chatham Road? The cause of the paranormal phenomena on Blue Bell Hill remains open for speculation. Regardless of the reasons, the ghosts of Blue Bell Hill continue to waylay Kent commuters.

Dead Man on Dug Hill Road

The story of the ghost of Dug Hill Road takes us to the southwest tip of Illinois more than 100 years ago, when the cannons of the Civil War were still roaring across the nation. It was late in the evening and two Union Army deserters, sickened and demoralized by the death around them, were making their way west down Dug Hill Road, intent on leaving the war behind them. The bloody contest had not yet been decided, but both of them had seen enough to decide that victory for either North or South wasn't worth the carnage of the war. Nothing was.

Taking the trail west, the men only traveled at night, careful to avoid the cities and towns of southern Illinois. They were dangerous men. The punishment for desertion was death, and although these two ex-soldiers were weary of killing, they would not hesitate at turning their guns against anyone who tried to arrest them. More than any-thing else, they were determined to live; that was why they were risking their lives, creeping across Illinois to get to the western territories. They wanted to flee the East and its blood-soaked battlefields.

The two deserters moved quietly down Dug Hill Road, staying out of the full moon's light by walking along the heavy bush on the side of the road. Besides the sounds of crickets and their boots on the dirt, the night was com-pletely still. The pair had made it across Illinois without being seen by a single man, woman or child, and had come to equate silence with safety. On this summer night, this silence was about to be broken.

They both froze when the sound of a horse's hooves approached them. Disappearing noiselessly into the bushes, the two men laid low and waited for whoever was behind them to pass. Before long, they heard the sound of a wagon's wheels. Two horses, one wagon, both men thought to themselves as the sound grew closer.

The next moment, the wagon was right in front of them. They saw a lone Union military officer in a wagon steering two horses down the road. In the clear moonlight they could make out the man's rank; he was a provost mar-shal, a senior officer of the military police. A man of his rank would preside over their court martial if they should ever be apprehended. The two deserters grinned and looked at each other in the darkness, both appreciating the irony of their potential executioner unknowingly riding right in front of them—and completely at their mercy.

And then they noticed the officer's horses. The two Union mounts looked better fed than the two men were, and once again they had the same thought. They were near the Missouri line, but there was still a lot of ground to cover if the men hoped to make it into Kansas. Two horses would definitely help them make it there quicker. Again, the two deserters looked at each other in the darkness. Both knew the other's thought. One of the men made the decision, nodding at the officer on the road and slowly running his index finger across his throat. The other man nodded.

In the next instant, the two men charged out of the bush, boarding the provost marshal's wagon before he knew what was going on. The officer registered the gleam of a knife in the moonlight and his hand went for his revolver, but it was too late. One of the deserters pulled the marshal down while the other slit his throat. The work was over in less than a second, completed with brutal efficiency. Neither man enjoyed it; they were trained killers and this was a matter of survival.

Pushing the marshal off the wagon before he was dead, the two men whipped the horses into a gallop and were gone. The Union officer lay alone in a pool of his own blood, his last thoughts spent contemplating the bright face of the full moon. His body was found by a local who was driving down the road the very next day, and the officer was promptly given a state burial. As for the two deserters, there is no record of how they fared in the West or even if they got there at all.

Although the two men vanished from the historical record, the provost marshal who met his end on Dug Hill Road has lingered well past his time, constantly reminding Union County residents in southern Illinois of the crime that occurred on Dug Hill Road. Or it might be more accurate to say that some part of the officer has remained behind on the spot where he was killed, much to the dismay of those commuters who have had the misfortune of running into him.

He was first spotted by an elderly farmer a few days after he was buried, lying in the exact same position that he was originally found: sprawled in a dark pool of his own blood, staring blankly at the sky above him. The war was not yet over, and the old man assumed that he was looking at another casualty of the conflict. Getting off his wagon to see if there was anything he could do, the farmer had not walked far when the corpse slowly began to vanish, becoming transparent right in front of him. He hadn't made it another five paces before the figure had faded into nothingness.

It was the first of many such sightings on Dug Hill Road. Over the years, the same apparition was reported countless times. Residents of Jonesboro, about five miles east of the scene of the murder, have long accepted the presence of the ghost on the nearby thoroughfare. He was there when horses provided transportation and he continues to be spotted today in the age of automobiles. Indeed, it seems that the ghost of the dead marshal is seen now more than ever, even though Dug Hill Road is now a paved section of Highway 146 and the Civil War has long run its course.

Not only is the body of the dead officer now seen on the road, but on many occasions late-night commuters have spotted a phantom wagon being pulled by two horses along the shoulder of the highway, slowly making its way west towards the Mississippi River. It is obvious to awestruck motorists that this is not a typical buggy, for it glows with an ethereal silver light and there is no driver steering it. The horses move on their own, proceeding slowly in their 19th-century harnesses. Those drivers who have stopped alongside the spectral wagon to get a closer look claim they can hear the sound of the horses' hooves on the road. The plodding pace continues as the wagon slowly begins to fade into nothingness. After about 20 yards, the wagon begins to fade away and the sound of the hooves becomes faint, as if coming from a great distance. A moment later, the wagon and horses vanish, leaving motorists on Highway 146 staring into the empty night.

3
Haunted Bridges

Most of us probably don't think about it when we are crossing them, but bridges are one of the most common sites of suicides, construction fatalities and lethal car accidents. Murderers have buried dead bodies underneath them or thrown bodies over the rails. In the past, when a gallows was unavailable, the authorities have even hanged their criminals from them. It is little wonder, then, that bridges are also a major focal point for the spirits of the dead. So much so that one might conclude bridges don't only serve motorists in crossing obstacles, but also assist the dead when they cross back into the land of the living.

The Van Sant Bridge

Van Sant Bridge can be found on Covered Bridge Road just off Highway 32 in Bucks County. The structure is tucked away within the verdant Pennsylvanian woodland, halfway between the town of New Hope and Washington Crossing Historic Park, a stone's throw from the Delaware River. Its pointed gable, stone embankments and wooden walls have been part of the local landscape since 1875, when the bridge was constructed to span Pidcock Creek. Although the bridge was built by 19th-century Pennsylvanians for transportation, those who cast eyes on Van Sant Bridge today have difficulty seeing the old structure solely for its practical purposes.

For many motorists who stumble upon the bridge, the sight of such an archaic overpass rising in the middle of the countryside inspires a sense of wonder. Almost invariably, these people slow down to take a close look at the structure, intently staring in much the same way observers might take in a museum artifact. Then there are those afflicted with nostalgia, who see the bridge as a representation of a rural golden age, when covered bridges could be found all over the northeast states. But warm thoughts are the last things on the minds of many others, who experience only a deep, irrational fear when staring into the gaping maw of Van Sant.

Strange stories about the Van Sant have been circulating for as long as anyone can remember. Motorists, hikers and paranormal investigators have all had strange and unsettling encounters on the old overpass. For many, these unsettling experiences have occurred in broad daylight, the moment the bridge becomes visible on the road. It is often no more than a feeling, a fierce sense of foreboding that grows ever stronger as the observer approaches the overpass. Those who have ignored this feeling and continued on through Van Sant's wooden tunnel have claimed that the sense of imminent danger increases dramatically within. It lasts for only a few seconds, but is so potent that those who have experienced it emerge from the other end profoundly unsettled.

Although there have been a variety of descriptions about the experiences within the tunnel, most people speak of a malevolent presence, intangible and angry, that looms within the darkness. If no one has ever been able to claim to have actually seen this mysterious entity in the daylight hours, all who have sensed it say that they felt certain that *it*—whatever *it* was—loathed them. More than one motorist driving through the Van Sant Bridge felt a very real danger—a sense that the invisible presence on the bridge was very close to committing a violent act. Yet the sense of dread passes as quickly as it comes, dissipating into nothingness the moment drivers emerge from the other end of the tunnel.

Those who cross at night, however, tend to have far more dramatic encounters with the presence that lurks within the Van Sant Bridge. Like so many of the other spirits that haunt the globe, the ghost over Pidcock Creek seems to grow stronger after the sun has gone down. The negative energy that emanates from the bridge during daylight hours seems to be compounded at night. Individuals put off by the sight of the bridge in the daytime are often too fearful to even approach the bridge after twilight.

Covered bridges often conceal dark haunted histories.

Where only the most psychically sensitive sense anything foreboding about the bridge when the sun is high, almost everyone crossing in the midnight hour have felt, at the very least, a tinge of fear.

Yet for so many others, the nocturnal events at the Van Sant Bridge have been far more memorable than vague premonitions and intangible fears. Some drivers have had their car engines seize up and their lights go out while in the middle of the tunnel. These unfortunates have experienced many horrible things while sitting helplessly within their stalled vehicles. One phenomenon commonly reported by individuals trapped in Van Sant Bridge at night is a drop in temperature so extreme that witnesses claim to be able to see their breath in the middle of July.

It does not stop there. Many people trying to restart their engines on the Van Sant Bridge claim that the silhouette of a man standing at the entrance to the tunnel suddenly appears in front of them. The sight of this man has filled some motorists with inexplicable terror, causing panicked drivers to stare fearfully at the outline of the man while repeatedly testing the ignition, desperately hoping to resurrect their engines with every turn of the key. Fear mounts until the figure at the entrance of the tunnel suddenly vanishes; moments later, headlights reactivate and inert engines spring back to life. The speed with which cars fly off the bridge in the following seconds— amid screeching tires and burning rubber—would inspire awe in drag racers. Those who have seen the ghost of the Van Sant Bridge rarely cross again.

Compared to others, however, these motorists get off relatively easily. A credulous few believe that the man standing at the end of the bridge might be able to help them start their cars and get out of their vehicles to ask for assistance. Judging by what happens next, it seems to be exactly what the black figure is waiting for. Within seconds, these helpless motorists are subjected to what can only be described as an attack. The figure lunges as soon as the driver gets out of the car, and a heartbeat later, the individual is beset by a terrible force.

Blows from ice-cold fists, a cold and crushing pressure squeezing breath from lungs, invisible hands raking frozen claws down the middle of the back—people have offered all sorts of descriptions for the supernatural assaults on the Van Sant Bridge. While there have been many different accounts of these attacks, the sheer terror of the experience remains consistent. Some try to retaliate, throwing panicked punches into the darkness, but no one claims to have connected with anything. Others dive back into their cars and lock the doors, while still others just run off the bridge as fast as their feet can take them, leaving their vehicles behind on the bridge. People taking refuge in their cars usually sit in frantic, heart-pounding fear for only a few minutes before their cars come back to life. And regardless of how long people wait before cautiously creeping back into their vehicles, the force that assaulted them never returns for another round.

Is the ghost of the Van Sant Bridge content with a single attack, perhaps convinced that it has done enough to ward the motorist away from ever crossing again? Or would the malevolent spirit prefer to do more harm, but is, for whatever reason, only capable of sustaining an assault for a short duration? Questions such as these have brought more than one paranormal society to the haunted bridge, intent on documenting and bringing to light the specter on the overpass. The work of these groups of supernatural enthusiasts has provided the public with the scant information now available on the mysterious phantom guarding the bridge over Pidcock Creek.

One of these groups discovered that those who walked over the bridge with a lit candle could cross unmolested.

Another paranormal society claimed that prayer offered the same protection from the belligerent ghost. Safeguarded under the aegis of light and prayer, investigators spent entire evenings on the Van Sant Bridge, where they recorded all sorts of bizarre phenomena. Sometimes they heard urgent whispering coming from all around them, harsh and incessant, hissing a message no one could quite make out. On other occasions, the sound of a man's groans have been heard drifting through the darkened tunnel; it has been described as a piteous, eerie sound, issued by some sad soul writhing in prodigious pain, fear or misery. But the most consistently reported nocturnal noise within the Van Sant Bridge comes from the wooden rafters in the ceiling. It is the sound of friction, of a rope rubbing heavily across the timber, as if a considerable weight was being hoisted up over one of the rafters. The rubbing sound usually lasts for about 10 seconds, replaced by an ominous creaking that continues for the better part of a minute.

From these investigations, it has been surmised that the ghost of the Van Sant Bridge might be a 19th-century criminal hanged from the rafters. Certainly, such impromptu executions, carried out by local lynch mobs across the country, were a common expression of 19th-century American "justice." So it could very well be that the terror over Pidcock Creek is the spirit of a Pennsylvanian murderer, horse thief or swindler, who was summarily tried, found guilty and put to death by some forgotten Bucks County vigilance committee.

Was he a mean man, guilty of the crimes charged against him, who continues to terrorize citizens in death as he did in life? Or was he an innocent man, wrongly accused and put to death, whose ongoing presence on Van Sant Bridge is some sort of supernatural revenge for his untimely end? No one is certain who the man on the bridge is or why he continues to terrorize people driving through Bucks County. But the ordeals of countless motorists driving over the bridge at night have made one thing clear—all who find themselves in the middle of the Van Sant would do well to stay in their cars. The mysterious man shrouded in the darkness has no intention of helping.

St. Andrew's Church Road

It appears as "Highway 4" on any road atlas or map of Maryland. Yet to many locals, the eight miles running east-west between Route 5 and Route 235 in St. Mary's County is known as St. Andrew's Church Road. A historic stretch of American thoroughfare, the road passes through some of the first lands settled by English immigrants; it is about an hour away from old St. Mary's City, the fourth English town established in North America and the first capital of Maryland.

Although it is registered as just another secondary highway, St. Andrew's Church Road stands apart from the myriad other roads tangled across the nation. For not only does it lie among the earliest European settlements in the United States, it is also haunted by three restless spirits that are either unable or unwilling to let go of the injustices of their pasts.

All these ghosts haunt a single bridge, about three miles east of where St. Andrew's Church Road splits off Route 5, in the dark, swampy marshland near the southern tip of Maryland. For many years now, motorists driving over this bridge at night have witnessed all sorts of strange things. Apparitions have been seen emerging from the darkness and into headlights. Eerie, ethereal sounds have been heard just over the noise of car engines—the sad pathetic cries of a distressed infant from the creek below, mingling with the immediate yet somehow distant screams of a terrified woman along the waters' banks.

Two separate tragedies, embedded in the local history, are believed to be responsible for the bizarre happenings on the bridge. The first took place sometime in the first half of the 19th century, when cotton was king of the South, and the Maryland countryside rang with the sounds of slave gangs working the fields. A slave owner with particularly cruel inclinations lived near the bridge on St. Andrew's Church Road. By all accounts, he was one of the worst men south of the Pennsylvania border. He was a drunken, violent, egocentric lout, who didn't understand a thing about the world around him and smelled worse than a hog barn. While Marylanders were free to shun his company, and often did, the slaves who belonged to this dissolute slob had no such luxury. These unfortunate men and women were bound to him by the property laws of the state and suffered all the pains that came with such association.

He was mercilessly cruel to the slaves on his plantation. He worked them past the point of exhaustion, kept them underfed and was liberal with his use of the whip, doling out lashes for any and every transgression. On bad days, slaves would be whipped beyond comprehension if they made eye contact with their master. His enmity was a horrible burden to bear, and he gave it freely to everyone around him. But those he took a liking to had it even worse.

One young slave became the subject of his lustful obsession. The very day he purchased her, he gave orders to have special quarters built for her, apart from where the rest of the slaves slept. He gave her the lightest work duties, charging her only to keep his house clean, while the rest of the slaves toiled through the backbreaking day in the fields. She dined at every meal, and he made sure she had a wardrobe that was as well stocked as any free-woman's.

Such privileged treatment, however, did not come without a price. Every evening, the cruel man paid her a visit, during which he would take his prurient recompense for the luxuries she enjoyed. The visits caused the woman to curse her lot on the plantation, even as the other slaves died from overwork and malnutrition. She would have gratefully traded places with any of the other field workers. Yet such a choice was not hers, so she bore the indignity of her station as best she could. She did not receive any comfort from the other slaves on the plantation; in fact, her privileged position earned her the envy of the others, adding the burden of isolation to her shame. Night after night, year after year, the woman was forced to submit to the lewd demands of her master, utterly alone, until one day something inside her snapped.

It happened on a night like any other. The work was done for the day, the sun had set and most of the slaves were sound asleep. The plantation patriarch, more than a little drunk, walked into his favorite slave's bedchamber, smiling at her through the darkness as he approached her.

She struck when he was an arm's length away; the young slave slit her master's throat with a kitchen knife she had stolen from his home. The old man fell with a look of utter disbelief on his face, always assuming that his captive mistress was thankful for his attention. She didn't say a single word to him as she ran from her quarters, into the night and away from the plantation, leaving her hated master to die in a pool of his own blood.

Whatever plans the young woman had for a new life as a freewoman were crushed after that night. A lynch mob caught up with her on St. Andrew's Church Road. White southerners never reacted well when a slave murdered a master, and the pleas of the black woman fell on deaf ears. Without a thought to the tortured years in her master's service, the lynch mob walked her to the bridge on St. Andrew's Church Road, shot her in the head and threw her into the creek. So ended her short-lived tenure as a freewoman.

As tragic as the young slave's story is, another event that took place on the St. Andrew's Church Road bridge merits comparison. The story occured a century later, in 1945, just after the Second World War ended. A local woman living near St. Andrew's Church Road was one of the millions of joyful Americans expecting a loved one to return safely from the conflict. She was especially glad because the man whom she had missed for the last three years was her husband, and she had a two-year-old baby boy who had not seen his father yet. The phone call came from the town of Hollywood, about five miles north of the farmhouse in which she lived. It was her husband. He had just arrived in town and was coming home.

Her heart raced with joy as she ran out into the back-yard to grab her son. Too excited to wait for her husband at home, the woman jogged out onto St. Andrew's Church Road with her boy in her arms. She stopped when she reached the bridge, listening eagerly for his approach. Her husband was just as thrilled as she was. Driving a car he had just purchased, he was flying down Maryland's back-roads with barely restrained joy, the promise of his future stretching before him like a golden horizon. He made the tight turn on St. Andrew's Church Road just before the bridge and barreled onto the overpass. That was when he saw his wife holding his boy in her arms.

She was standing on the middle of the road, staring at her husband through the car windshield, unable to grasp what was about to happen. By the time he hit the brakes, it was too late. His car skidded across the bridge and struck the woman he loved, killing her instantly. The boy sailed out of her arms, over the bridge railing and into the creek below. Authorities searched the stream for weeks after the tragedy, but no trace was ever found.

But they heard him. They heard him later the same night for the first time, and succeeding generations heard him for years to come. His plaintive weeping was heard down the creek, competing with the sound of the babbling waters. He cried for hours that evening, and those who heard him were overjoyed, believing that the boy had survived the gruesome accident and was lost somewhere in the bush. But the nocturnal search turned up nothing. They heard the crying the following night, and their hopes were bolstered again, but their frantic hunt in the dark was once again in vain. The boy cried every night for the next two weeks, driving rescue workers into a state of near frenzy; they combed the creek and the surrounding bush, but couldn't find the elusive boy. Finally, after a month had passed, they gave up the search. The crying child hadn't been heard for a week so everyone assumed the worst.

That wasn't the last they heard of the boy. The sound of his weeping returned one evening a few weeks later and continued to be heard on and off throughout the years, impelling locals to dub the waterway Cry Baby Creek. Even today, years after the boy's father moved away, the baby's gentle wailing can be heard from the bridge on St. Andrew's Church Road. Something about the childish sobs fills most people with an intangible fear, and the majority who hear the crying evacuate the bridge as quickly as they can.

Yet there are many who ignore the mortal chill that usually accompanies the sound of the childish wailing and look over the edge of the bridge. Those who do are treated to an eerie sight. For down below, along the banks of the stream, witnesses have seen a bedraggled young woman, hunched over and looking frantically through the bush, searching for something of immeasurable value. She is never visible for more than a minute, vanishing suddenly right before astonished observers, who blink vapidly in the suddenly silent night. The apparition appeared often enough to set local tongues wagging, and it was not long before storytellers and paranormal enthusiasts formulated an explanation for the strange phenomenon—based on the tragedy that occurred on the bridge in 1945.

Some reach back even further to explain their experiences on St. Andrew's Church Road bridge. These are the motorists who have come to a screeching halt on the overpass, stopped by a grisly and terrifying figure lit in the pale glow of their car headlights. She is a black woman, dressed in tattered and bloody 19th-century finery. She stares blankly at horrified witnesses while blood flows freely from a dime-sized hole in her head. She stands there for a short time only—two heartbeats, maybe three—before vanishing as quickly as she came.

Few have had much doubt about the identity of this apparition, which started appearing shortly after the tragedy in 1945. The story of the lynched black woman was one of the county's most well-known folktales, and her appearance on St. Andrew's Church Road made a strange sort of sense to paranormal enthusiasts. Why she waited a century to start appearing, however, is another question.

Did the tragic car accident somehow exert some sort of supernatural force that pulled her spirit back onto the bridge to relive her own tragedy? Is her ghost an expression of sympathy? A reminder of the racial travesties of the past? Or perhaps, on a darker note, a supernatural articulation of vengeance? Could it be that the murdered woman died with such a hatred for the white Southerners who oppressed her that some part of her has remained on the bridge, looking for revenge? If such is indeed the case, drivers should be aware that the bridge over Cry Baby Creek may very well be cursed. They would do well to be extra careful when crossing the haunted overpass.

The Char-Man

He finds his gruesome origins in 1948 in the mountains around the Ojai Valley, California. During the summer, a raging bush fire had gone out of control in Ventura County, burning a smoking black swath through the forest above the town of Ojai and destroying a large number of homes in the valley. At the time, he was only a child, no older than 13, living in an isolated cabin with his father. We can only wonder at the horror of the experience, especially for a child who could only watch as his entire world was literally turned into a roaring inferno.

The boy's experiences in that horrific blaze are shrouded in mystery, for no one was there to witness how father and son dealt with the destruction of their home. But the sight of the aftermath provided evidence enough of what happened. Firefighters stumbled onto the grisly scene a few days after the fire had burned itself out; what they saw on the mountain where the small cabin used to stand was so bad that it burned itself into the local memory, becoming one of Ojai's most infamous folktales.

Beside the destroyed log cabin was the body of a grown man. It lay on the ground with each limb lashed to a stake with a metal wire. It appeared the man had been tortured and flayed. The boy was nowhere to be found.

It was surmised that the combination of the fire and the loss of his father had driven the boy mad, and somehow, in an inexplicable fit, he stripped the skin off his father's dead body. How the boy survived the fire and where he had gone was anyone's guess, but the general assumption was that if he was indeed alive, he must have been badly burned and would not be alive for long. For a few years, at least, this theory stuck.

And then bizarre sightings began to be reported along the Ojai Valley's Signal Street. The local police started to receive late night phone calls from breathless Californians who had just seen a beastly humanoid creature leap on the road. It was illuminated by their headlights one moment and vanished from the side of the road the next. Others told of taking their cars up to a local lookout point for some quiet time, only to have their vehicles assaulted by a man-monster that grunted and roared as it pounded on their windshields. Some were unfortunate enough to get clear glimpses of the mysterious creature; occasionally it got close enough to vehicles' headlights for motorists to make out the details of its face or it would stop frozen in the cone of a nocturnal pedestrian's flashlight before bolting off into the woods.

The descriptions of the creature are fairly consistent. Dressed in tattered old clothing, it is always seen wearing the same ripped and dirty red windbreaker, limping heavily on one leg and bent low under some invisible weight. But it is the creature's face that causes the most alarm. Those who have gotten close enough describe a man's face horribly disfigured by madness and fire. The creature's charred and mutilated visage has earned it the nickname "Char-Man."

By the mid 1960s, Char-Man was something of a local celebrity. A great many local Ojai teenagers had seen him during nightly forays into the surrounding mountains, and stories about Char-Man encounters and attacks were legion. Police took to patrolling the area, just as concerned about keeping order among the curious teenagers going into the mountains as they were about any possible confrontations with the mysterious mountain-dweller. Sightings of the Char-Man continued to increase as more and more people went up into the mountains looking for him.

Never spotted during daylight hours, the creature seemed to be active only at night—a quick flash of movement through the woods, a grunt and bellow from the darkness, a split-second appearance in the light of a curiosity-seeker's lantern. Weekend after weekend, the hills between Signal Street and Daly Road teemed with Ojai youth combing the brush in order to spot the Char-Man. More often than not, they were rewarded. And then, abruptly and without warning, the sightings stopped. It took the local kids a few weeks to figure out that the creature had disappeared. Some of the more stubborn teenagers continued their weekend forays into the woods, but after a few more months of silence, even the most ardent thrill-seekers gave up on Char-Man.

The next couple years passed without a single incident with Char-Man, and the horror of Ventura County seemed to be destined for the canon of local folklore. The Ojai kids, now a few years older, took to telling their Char-Man anecdotes as if they were ancient history. He became a commonly circulated ghost story around campfires across the state. There were many different Char-Man stories, most of them based on individual encounters with the sylvan monstrosity; but they all opened with the same horrible introduction, about a boy and his father caught in a raging fire. The end of the story, however, allowed much room for interpretation. "He just disappeared one day," raconteurs would say to fascinated listeners, "vanished without a trace."

Ventura County residents were convinced they had seen the last of the Char-Man. That was until a hot July night in 1967, when a group of five teenagers loafing about on Creek Road Bridge in Camp Comfort County Park, a few miles south of Ojai, had a terrifying encounter in the dark. It was a Saturday night, and the five boys were hanging out on the bridge. They had been there for a while, with their car parked on the shoulder of Creek Road with the hazard lights on. Intent on expressing their adolescent restlessness as concisely as possible, the boys leaned off the edge of the bridge and hollered at the sky; they threw rocks into the darkness and roared at the creek; they pushed each other around and yelled into one another's faces. As far as they were concerned, their night couldn't have been going any better.

That was when their revelry was interrupted by a sound on the opposite end of the bridge. It was a strange hyena-like grunt somewhere between animal and human, a completely foreign noise that none of them had ever heard before. Turning their gazes down the length of the bridge, the boys saw him standing there. Only his silhouette was visible in the night. He was stooped over, misshapen by a hideous stump that grew from his back; and although it was dark, it was obvious that he was breathing heavily, as if he had just run a great distance.

The boys instinctively began backing up towards their car. None of them knew who the man was, but they could sense that, whoever he was, he didn't mean well. Slowly, the uninvited guest stalked onto the bridge, matching the boys' backwards steps with his own awkward, limping movement. "Who are you?" asked one of the boys, his voice sounding small and scared in the tense silence. "What do you want?"

Another one of the kids spoke up, his voice barely above a whisper. "It's the Char-Man."

The disfigured man shrieked and lunged forward. In the next moment, he was coming at them, moving with a speed that startled all of them. Frightened out of their wits, the five boys turned and ran for the car, with the sound of the Char-Man's lopsided footfalls right behind them. Four of the teenagers made it into the car, slamming the doors behind them and starting the engine before noticing that one of their number was still outside.

His name was Richard Muckner, and he was no more than six feet away from the car when he felt a powerful blow across his back. Stumbling forward onto his knees, he tried to get up when he was struck again. The Char-Man drove his fist into the youngster's lower back, knocking him flat on the ground. Richard was barely able to register the pain when his assailant hauled him up by the back of his jacket. On his feet and face to face with the Char-Man, Richard began punching into the darkness. A close flailing match prevailed for the next few minutes until Richard's friends finally reacted, turning on the car headlights on the bridge and charging out of the car to help their friend.

The Char-Man was gone before they got there. Shrinking at the car's headlights as if they caused him pain, he dropped Richard, spun around and ran from the scene, vanishing into the darkness. Muckner collapsed in an exhausted heap when his friends reached him. The confrontation with the Char-Man had left its marks: the sheepskin jacket he wore had been torn into ribbons, he had multiple bruises across his back and arms and the first signs of an ugly shiner were spreading over his left eye. But these were all wounds that would quickly heal; the most lasting damage was psychological. The sight of the Char-Man's face illuminated by the car headlights stuck with him for months after his physical injuries healed. He would not easily forget the long creases of fire-blackened tissue stretching across the man's face or the horribly rotted teeth poking through his snarling lips, which were split open and covered with warts. If there was such thing as a monster on earth, Richard Muckner was certain he had fought one.

After the encounter with the Char-Man on Creek Road Bridge, local fascination with the Char-Man returned, and over the next few months Camp Comfort County Park was packed on the weekends. There were many additional sightings. He was spotted most often along the banks of the creek under Creek Road Bridge, visible from a distance for only a few seconds, before he realized he was being watched and would promptly limp out of sight.

The furor over the Char-Man lasted for a few years into the early 1970s, until sightings began decreasing dramatically. And then, one day, he vanished again, just as he had done years ago. There were no more sightings of the limping man in the woods, no accounts of spine-tingling howls drifting down Old Creek Road, and as much as Char-Man hunters were willing to dramatize the accounts of their forays into Camp Comfort, even their fertile imaginations were thwarted by the silence in the woods. Once again, the Char-Man disappeared without a trace.

This time, it seemed that he was gone for good. One year followed another, until over two decades had come and gone without a single peep from the horror of Ventura County. He had been all but forgotten by locals, a nostalgic subject that Ojai baby boomers talked about alongside the athletic feats of their high school days. No one believed they would see, or hear, from the Char-Man again.

And then, on a hot July evening in 1997, he struck again. Two Ojai residents were returning home from a day trip to Los Angeles. The sun had set a few hours previous when they pulled off Highway 33 onto Old Creek Road. Slowing down on the darkened path, the pair was almost out of Camp Comfort Park when a humpbacked man suddenly appeared in their headlights. They had just rounded a wide bend in the road when they spotted him; he was crouched low, picking at something on the road, and the driver slammed on the brakes to avoid hitting him. A second later, the man was up on his feet, limping towards the car with amazing speed. Every warped detail in his face stood out as he ran towards the light. His skin was a formless mass of fleshy wrinkles, heavily scarred by hideous burns. He issued a horrible scream as he came at them, his toothless mouth gaping in an expression that could have been agony or rage. The driver didn't wait to find out. Hitting the gas hard, he dodged the approaching man and sped all the way into Ojai, not looking into the rearview mirror once.

Ever since that summer night, people have been reporting sightings of the Char-Man on Old Creek Road. He is usually seen on the bridge in Camp Comfort, either loping along the shoulder of the road in the glow of a car's headlights or dashing off the road and disappearing before an oncoming vehicle passes him. Many motorists, concerned that he might be an old man in need of assistance, have stopped their vehicles hoping to lend a hand. Given what ensues when these good Samaritans stop their cars, it is safe to assume that the Char-Man does not need or want assistance. So all motorists driving through Ventura County at night should be warned: think twice before stopping for a hunched old man on the side of the road. It might be the Char-Man, and he has not softened in his old age.

Spirits at Sachs Covered Bridge

The sun was setting on a beautiful summer's day in Adams County, Pennsylvania. George Rush and John McDermott were standing against their parked car, just off Waterworks Road, engaged in animated conversation over the day's events. Rush and McDermott were two Civil War buffs who had just spent the entire day at Gettysburg National Military Park. Neither of them had been to the battlefield before, and both had a lot of ideas and observations they wanted to unload on each other.

For the most part, the pair was heedless of the lush Pennsylvanian landscape that surrounded them: the

Sachs Covered Bridge in Adams County, Pennsylvania

midsummer greenery, the lazy waters of Marsh Creek, the antiquated covered bridge that spanned it a dozen yards from where they stood. George and John had intentionally ended their day at the Sachs Covered Bridge, where over half of General Lee's army had retreated after the battle, but the bridge itself was a minor addendum to the things they had seen that day.

"You really get an idea of how skilled those sharp-shooters at Devil's Den must have been," George Rush was saying, "picking off Union soldiers on the crest of Little Round Top like that."

"Yeah," John said. "Seeing the dimensions of the battle-field firsthand really changes the way I picture the battle."

"I was surprised at how steep the slopes of Little Round Top were," George said. "I mean, we were sucking wind just *walking* up that hill. What would it have been like for the Confederates who had to run up it, loaded down with gear and under heavy fire?"

John McDermott was about to add something to his friend's observation when a loud crack sounded from the covered bridge behind them, shattering the silence of the quiet evening and startling both men badly. The next minute passed in exaggerated silence, as if all of nature seemed suddenly focused on the Sachs Bridge. "What the hell was that?" John finally said, as surprised as he was frightened.

"I don't know," George said, whispering. "It sounded like it could've been a rifle shot." Both men were tense, standing instinctively on the balls of their feet, poised to bolt, staring intently at Sachs Bridge. Now that the bridge absorbed all their attention, they wondered how they did not notice it before. Its wooden trusses criss-crossed along the tunnel's interior, forming intricate lattice walls that let the setting sun's light into the tunnel in triangular patterns. Its high roof and enormous entrance somehow expressed a vague displeasure at the pair's presence. The bridge, anchored by two stone embankments on either side, suddenly looked sentient, and at that moment, Rush and McDermott were possessed by an uncomfortable certainty that the bridge was doing all it could to shake off its moorings and lunge at them.

They both stood there, holding their breath for what seemed like long moments, silently staring at the crossing, unable to grasp what exactly made the bridge seem so sinister. For a minute, maybe two, the silence weighed heavy and the bridge seemed to breathe.

When the second gunshot went off, both men dove into the car in frantic silence, pulling away from the bridge as quickly as their car could take them. So went two more petrified witnesses from the Sachs Bridge, taking with them yet another bizarre tale of the old covered bridge.

If they had done their research before coming to Gettysburg, George and John would have known that such strange phenomena have been occurring at the Sachs Covered Bridge for over a century. The bridge was built in 1852, connecting Cumberland Township to Freedom Township over swampy Marsh Creek. Located just southwest of Gettysburg, the bridge's timbers trembled and shook during the first three days of July 1863, when roaring cannons and rifles claimed the lives of 50,000 men in the most terrible battle in American history. The bridge, just behind the Confederate right flank, stood over a makeshift field hospital that was quickly flooded with Southern wounded; it also provided passage for defeated Confederates retreating southwest after the battle. Today, the bridge stands just outside Gettysburg National Military Park. Often overlooked by visiting Civil War buffs, it has become an attraction for a different sort of enthusiast.

Paranormal investigators, students of American folklore, psychics and curiosity seekers have all come to the Sachs Bridge over the years, hoping to witness the supernatural

Paranormal phenomena reported in and around the bridge include eerie gunshots and apparitions of hanging bodies.

goings-on said to occur there. For many of these visitors, trips to the bridge were not made in vain. One of the most well-documented paranormal occurrences was witnessed by George Rush and John McDermott. The gunshots on the Sachs have been reported by numerous visitors and are heard most often at dusk, just before the sun dips out of sight. The other phenomenon is visual, not auditory, and what it lacks in acoustic effect, it makes up in horrific imagery.

Many people have mistaken them for three large potato sacks, hanging from three separate ropes on the Cumberland Township side of the bridge, put there, perhaps, by local pranksters with too much time on their hands. Each of them is suspended about two feet from the ground, silhouetted by the night's sky as they sway gently, causing the trusses of the bridge to creak and groan. The shapes look ominous at first sight, but those that approach closer are struck by much more than the shivers. When they are about 25 yards away, witnesses realize that the objects hanging from the tunnel entrance aren't potato sacks. At such a distance human attributes become visible: dangling limbs, swollen fingers, lifeless heads attached to grotesquely elongated necks, strung up to the bridge's rafters by hangman's nooses. How would most of us react to the sight of three dead men hanging right before us?

More often than not, terrified witnesses turn around and run out of the bridge, perhaps issuing a series of frantic curses, with vague ideas of informing the authorities beginning to form in their minds. But those who cast a glance over their shoulders for a second look find themselves suddenly still, stopping in their tracks at the sight of the nothingness behind them. The bolder observers who do not run, but approach the hanging figures to take a closer look, actually witness the three dead bodies blink out of existence before their very eyes. No one knows why these hanging corpses materialize, when they appear or how long they stay for.

Indeed, very little has been written on the history of Sachs Bridge. It is true that it was in close proximity to the Battle of Gettysburg, and that it served as a path of escape for retreating Confederates. Does this fact explain the gunshots that have been heard coming from the bridge? Paranormal enthusiasts often claim that the historic Civil War battle was so traumatic that the battle-field is permeated by supernatural phenomena—spiritual expressions of the loss and horror felt by the participants of the three-day battle. Could the trauma of war extend to the Sachs Bridge, where thousands of retreating soldiers each struggled with the cost of the lost battle? Unlike the Union Army, the Confederates did not have the elation of victory to buoy the horrible thought of the human price that was paid.

As for the hanging bodies, it is anyone's guess why they appear. The only other recorded fact in the history of the Sachs Bridge concerns an extended deluge that washed over Adams County in the summer of 1996. Marsh Creek rose under the heavy downfall, pulling the old bridge off its foundations and carrying it downstream for about 100 yards. Almost immediately, a restoration effort was undertaken to save the Sachs Bridge. The bridge was put back in its rightful position within a year, saved by county, government and private donations.

The flood, however, hardly explains the hanging bodies. No one was reported to have drowned when Marsh Creek rose, and there were no casualties when the bridge was restored. Yet the dangling apparitions persist, spawning conjecture, legends and lies. Many theories have been advanced: vigilantes hanging local horse thieves in the middle of the night, victims of a silent-but-deadly family feud, murders committed by some solitary killer who wandered Adams County a long time ago.

While the mystery of the Sachs Bridge might remain unsolved, the strange sights and sounds recur on the pedestrian bridge at nightfall, providing tourists, locals and investigators with yet another haunted covered bridge in the northeastern United States.

Emily's Bridge

The small town of Stowe is tucked away in northern Vermont, where the lush Green Mountains color the landscape in vibrant hues. Situated on beautiful Highway 100, the peaceful town hardly seems the kind of place where the demons of the past might return—until, that is, one takes a trip down Gold Brook Road a few miles out of town. Here, where the waters of Gold Brook intersect the narrow country road, the feeling in the air suddenly changes. Many have described it as a slight shift in the light, where everything somehow seems to grow a few shades darker, even on the brightest of summer days. Others claim to have felt a sudden drop in temperature as they approach the country brook. It is said to be a strange kind of cold, one that seeps through every kind of clothing.

These natural aberrations recur without fail in the area immediately around the covered bridge spanning Gold Brook. Over the years, innumerable witnesses have claimed to feel a sudden chill in the air and the darkening of the landscape the moment the bridge comes into sight. The infamous bridge never looks welcoming. Indeed, the old wooden structure, with its dark lumber, pointed gable and gaping tunnel, somehow conveys a sense of hostility, as if it would *prefer* that no traffic run through it. While this feeling is more pronounced on some days than on others, people who approach the covered bridge after the

The histories of New England's covered bridges give rise to many fascinating ghost stories.

sun has gone down tend to report especially strong sensations, as if the unholy force that possesses the old bridge grows stronger during the evening hours. It is then, when the pointed roof of the covered bridge is silhouetted against a dark night's sky, that the bridge seems to take on a life of its own. The experiences of those who have crossed the bridge at night have transformed the old structure from a creepy historical landmark into one of Vermont's most lasting legends.

Her name was Emily Smith, a young woman who lived in the village of Stowe during the latter half of the 19th century. The favorite daughter of one of the town's more respected families, Emily grew up getting whatever she wanted—until, that is, she fell victim to forbidden love. The young man's name has been forgotten by history, but it is likely that there weren't many who would have bothered to remember it even while he was alive. He was an untouchable, a man who had lived on the wrong side of the tracks, unsuited, unworthy of a self-respecting woman's attention. Or so the Smith family believed. Yet despite her upbringing and her family's high expectations, Emily fell in love with the underprivileged young man and, with a passion reserved for the young, was determined to make the relationship work. It would prove her undoing.

Their affair continued in secret for a few months before the couple decided they would marry, arranging to meet on the Gold Brook Bridge on an upcoming evening. They would elope, leave behind the difficult circumstances of their hometown to start fresh somewhere else, far away from the world they knew. Or so Emily thought. When the appointed night came, she sneaked out of her home, taking the family's best horse and enough of her parent's valuables to establish the couple in another town. She departed in the middle of the moonlit night, but there was no one waiting for her when she arrived at the bridge. The minutes passed, one after another, but there was no sign of her lover. Emily waited in the dark recesses of the bridge tunnel, straining to hear a sound above the creek that flowed underneath. Nothing.

Long before the first traces of dawn began to appear in the night sky, Emily was worried. She couldn't understand or accept the heartbreak of the situation. She had robbed her family to be with a man who abandoned her.

It was all over by the time the sun rose over the Green Mountains. Early-morning travelers making their way into town were the first to witness the aftermath of the tragedy. The timbers of the covered bridge creaked ominously under a morbid weight, while the horse Emily had stolen grazed on a nearby patch of grass. She was found hanging from one of the rafters inside the covered bridge, swaying gently on the end of a rope, her broken neck stretched to grotesque proportions.

From that day on, the bridge over Gold Brook was known as Emily's Bridge. And while no one knows what became of the young woman's lover after she died, subsequent events at Gold Brook Bridge have led many to believe that Emily herself has developed a strong attachment to the covered bridge in the afterlife. For not long after the poor woman was buried, people began to report strange experiences at the crossing.

Many of those crossing the bridge during daylight hours spoke of an intangible menace in the area. Others swore that the bridge itself somehow seemed alive, silently glowering at any approaching traffic with a frightening intensity. But Emily's Bridge made an even stronger impression on those unfortunate individuals who found themselves crossing the structure at night.

Commuters piloting horse-drawn wagons through the darkness of the tunnel were alerted to danger by their horses' reactions. Many of these animals would suddenly resist venturing into the darkness of the covered bridge, moving forward only after firm encouragement at the end of a whip. The darkness that enclosed both beast and passenger once they were under the roof was unnaturally absolute. As the carriage made its way across the creaky boards, the blighted structure did its worst.

Some heard a woman's hysterical wailing coming from every direction within the pitch black of the tunnel. Others claimed to hear incoherent babbling, high-pitched and frantic, in which a single, barely discernible, question punctuates a mad cacophony of random syllables. "Where is he?" the frantic voice asks of the oblivious darkness and the terrified soul who is passing through.

Then there were those who actually felt the ice-cold touch of something foreign as they moved over the bridge. Wagon drivers felt as if they had struck someone who was hanging from the roof's beams, and the frigid skin was a person's feet brushing their faces as they drove by. The moment the icy flesh pressed against them, the space within the tunnel was suddenly filled with a single, bloodcurdling scream, whereupon horse and master fled as quickly as possible. The instant the screaming began, however, the drivers felt ice-cold hands close around their throats in the remaining time the drivers were in the tunnel, relinquishing their grip only when their carriages were clear of the tunnel and into the suddenly quiet night. Those who had these dramatic experiences later discovered, invariably, that long scratches had been carved into the sides of their vehicles, as if a being of immeasurable strength had raked its fingernails across the surface. These dramatic experiences, which recurred over the years, cemented Emily's Bridge in the canon of local folklore.

These supernatural incidents did not cease when automobiles replaced horses on the roads of Vermont. To this day, motorists crossing Stowe's covered bridge at night continue to have terrifying experiences. People speak of feeling something bump and drag against the roofs of their cars, while passersby claim to have seen strange points of light blinking on and off around the haunted structure. Strange wails, screams, the sensation of being choked—all these ghostly attacks have persisted on the cursed bridge over the years.

How long will Emily's tortured spirit remain on the bridge over Gold Brook? Does she tarry in the vain hope that her long-absent lover will eventually meet with her? Or is her ghost trapped on the covered bridge, unable to overcome the horrible trauma of the last moments of her mortal life? Whatever the case, Emily's Bridge continues to be a supernatural landmark of Vermont's countryside, terrorizing those travelers who happen upon the crossing late at night.

Keenan Bridge Afire

From the very beginning, there was something wrong with Keenan Bridge. It was built in 1927 to span the Monquart River just north of the community of Johnville, in Carlton County in western New Brunswick, Canada. Legend has it that one of the laborers working on the bridge's construction unearthed a human skull on the banks of the Monquart while laying the foundation for the overpass. At the time, it aroused mild curiosity but it was quickly forgotten as work progressed. Indeed, the grisly incident probably would have been forgotten altogether if not for the bizarre phenomena that began to occur soon after Keenan Bridge was completed.

The construction workers who built the bridge could only shudder when they were finished. It stood as something more than the mere sum of its parts. Its trusses, embankments, roof and tunnel seemed to emit a malevolent energy. All who looked on it had the uncomfortable feeling that they were somehow in danger. These early premonitions were confirmed when the bridge came into use.

The man who saw the apparition was a local farmer returning home from business in Johnville in a horse-drawn buggy. Reaching Keenan Bridge just as the sun was sinking behind the trees, the man had been paying only casual attention to the road. Suddenly, and for no reason he would ever be able to explain, he pulled his horses to a complete stop.

The farmer had never liked the look of the Monquart River crossing, but it never looked like this before. He sat silently and stared into the dwindling twilight, unable to pin down what it was about the bridge that was so unsettling. Then he became possessed by the disturbing feeling that the bridge was staring back at him, and it was not happy about what it saw. He was afraid. For a few moments, the farmer thought about turning back and taking another bridge across, but just as he was about to back up he felt ashamed at his irrational seizure of fear. Without another thought, the man put the whip to his horses and spurred them forward onto the wooden platform of the covered bridge. In the next instant, he was in the darkness under the bridge roof. The noise of his horses' hooves was exaggerated in the close confines of the tunnel. It was then that the heart-stopping terror seized him.

His first awareness of the woman's presence came with the horrifying sensation that he was not alone in the tunnel. He couldn't see her through the darkness and she didn't say anything to alert him of her presence, but he knew somehow that she was sitting next to him in his buggy. And he knew, beyond a shadow of a doubt, that she wasn't friendly.

Then the buggy was under the dusky sky again, and for a split second he saw her clearly in the early evening light. Although she appeared for less than an instant, visible only for the duration of a lightning streak, every detail of the female apparition was burned into the farmer's memory. Try as he might, he was never able to forget her, and over the course of his life he would describe her countless times to friends and strangers alike.

"She was white," the farmer would say, his voice barely above a whisper, "whiter than white, pale as a corpse or the bone of an animal. And her hair was long and straight, black as pitch and blowing all around her. She wore a heavy black dress, buttoned right up to her chin, and there was no mistaking her for anything but evil."

"It was in her eyes," the farmer swore. "The Devil was in her eyes. She smiled at me and I thought I saw the Devil. I was sure I was going to die."

But he did not die. As soon as the farmer's horse touched the opposite bank, the woman vanished into thin air, leaving the man alone in his buggy with a racing heart and a lifelong memory of evil.

So went the first of many encounters with the ghost of Keenan Bridge. She appeared to countless people over the years, frightening the life out of equestrians, carriage drivers and motorists alike. While those who encountered her had experiences that were similar enough, there was often some variation in the accounts. For instance, many people claimed that a woman's bloodcurdling wail filled the tunnel just before they emerged to find themselves sitting next to the ghoulish female. Others added a disquieting detail, stating that the woman who appeared in their vehicle as they crossed the bridge was actually headless. Although she was described bereft of any vocal cords in these accounts, she never failed to issue a horrible cry before vanishing right in front of terrified witnesses.

The phantom of Keenan Bridge haunted motorists through much of the 20th century, causing the bridge to become one of the haunted places in the province of New Brunswick. But it wasn't until the evening of May 3, 2001, that the bridge received national attention in Canada. Residents of Johnville were woken by the sound of sirens in the night as firefighters raced to put out the fire on the banks of the Monquart River. The surrounding forest was lit in orange and yellow by the roaring blaze raging on Keenan Bridge. The firemen worked throughout the night, but by morning nothing was left of the overpass but a pile of smoldering rubble.

Journalists and Johnville townsfolk crowded around the bridge that summer morning. It was just days before the community's annual church picnic, which was going to be dedicated to the historic Keenan Bridge. But it seems that there were some parties that may not have approved of the celebration. For evidence on the site led investigators to believe that arson was the cause of the fire, although no suspects were ever apprehended. While such mystery would have been sufficient to enshrine Keenan Bridge in the local folklore, it was a single photograph that a witness took of the smoldering ruins that turned the covered overpass into a front-page story in newspapers across the nation.

Among the bridge's smoking trusses, the amateur photographer had captured the long-storied ghost of Keenan Bridge on film. Her disembodied, semi-transparent head hovered over the ruins, staring directly into the camera. Her faded features were discernible enough to make out a head of dark hair, which seemed to be piled in a bun over her head, and a surprisingly callow complexion.

Ever since the bridge burned down, there hasn't been another sighting of the ghostly woman who once haunted it. She seems to have vanished completely, leaving countless unanswered questions behind her. For unlike other haunted bridges in North America, Keenan Bridge has no dark tragedy in its past. No bloodthirsty criminals were hanged by its rafters; there was never a fatal vehicle accident that occurred on the overpass; and no one died in the process of building the bridge.

The only possible explanation history provides is the skull the bridge builder dug up along the riverbank in 1927. While it was never determined who the skull belonged to or why it was there, most paranormal enthusiasts and folklorists have concluded that it belongs to the ghost of Keenan Bridge. Was she a murder victim forgotten by history? Perhaps from the nearby state of Maine? And where were the rest of her remains buried? A good number of sightings have her headless. Could she be the spirit of an angry woman, haunting the area where her head was buried?

As with many questions regarding the supernatural, any answer is speculation at best. But ever since the bridge was burnt down by unknown arsonists, these questions have been asked less and less. New Brunswick motorists driving along the Monquart River may rest easy knowing that whatever hatred the ghost had for the living seems to have dissipated. Then again, the bridge was not destroyed too long ago. Could it be that the ghost is only looking for another bridge to haunt? Only time will tell.

The Pitcher Man

His name was William Richardson. He was an American patriot living in the Goose River area of Camden, Maine, during the War of Independence. An ardent supporter of the revolution during the war, Richardson had put his property, finances and life in danger more than once during the eight-year conflict. So when the 13 colonies finally won independence in 1783, no man in the Goose River settlement was more ecstatic than William Richardson.

Word of the Treaty of Paris arrived by boat in Camden and reached Goose River a few short hours later. That same day, Richardson spread the word through the community that the finest celebration in the town's short history would be held in the burg's common rooms—all food and drink were on him. It was a celebration worthy of the birth of a nation. Practically everyone in the surrounding area showed up for the fête. Meat rotated on a spit and cups overflowed with ale and wine. Richardson took it on himself to make sure that there wasn't an empty mug in town and was seen walking through the tavern with two full pitchers in his hand, refilling everyone who needed it.

Throughout the Revolutionary War, the majority of people in Goose River fell on the side of independence. While there were some Loyalists in the countryside, Redcoats (or British soldiers) had regularly raided the town for supplies during the conflict, and whatever moderation prevailed in the town was destroyed by these harsh visits. One of these forays into Goose River got out of control, resulting in the town being put to the torch after soldiers made away with the locals' cattle and grain.

These memories were fresh in the minds of all. As a result, the citizens of Goose River celebrated the passing of the colonial tyranny with great enthusiasm—and no one more so than William Richardson. The patriarch of one of the town's leading families, he possessed considerable wealth, and so stood to lose the most when the Redcoats came through. This concern had plagued him almost daily for the last eight years, and now, suddenly, it was lifted.

Ecstatic and thoroughly inebriated, Richardson stumbled out of the tavern and onto the streets of the tiny settlement on the Atlantic. Worried that there were people in town who were not properly celebrating, Richardson wandered the streets of Goose River with a full pitcher in each hand. But the streets were deserted; everyone in town was at his party. So he decided to celebrate in the deserted town.

Taking the main street through the coastal settlement, Richardson raised his pitchers and drank to Goose River's health. He hollered at the buildings around him and the sky, joyously aware of all the possibilities that stretched out before the new republic. He eventually came to the bridge over Goose River, and was about to turn back when he saw three riders approaching in the darkness.

"Hey there, strangers!" Richardson called out to the men, raising his pitchers in the air. "Welcome to our humble town!"

He began walking across the bridge towards the three men, grinning with good cheer. As the riders got closer, Richardson made out that they were soldiers. Rifles were slung across their backs and sabers bounced in their scabbards along their horses' flanks. "Ahoy!" Richardson yelled when he saw these were fighting men. "Heroes of the Revolution! Minute Men for our great cause! Welcome, welcome!"

He broke into an awkward run, holding his two pitchers aloft, ale sloshing over the sides as he jogged across the bridge. "Here brothers, take, drink!" he yelled out offering the ale to the riders as they pulled up onto the bridge. The befuddled man didn't notice until the last minute that these men weren't smiling—in fact, they didn't look happy at all. That they were soldiers was obvious, but they weren't soldiers from the winning side.

The three Loyalists drew their horses up at the foot of the bridge, staring scornfully at the drunken man in front of them. "And this is what we're surrendering this land to," one of the riders said, nodding at the sloshed man standing there with two pitchers raised in the air.

"Vermin," said another, looking at William Richardson as if he were an enormous insect.

Richardson was far too drunk to react the way he ought to have, and although somewhere inside he knew he should be acting differently, he just stood there with a broad grin on his face, offering three of the enemy some ale. "Are you laughing at us, dog?" one of the soldiers asked Richardson.

Before he could utter any kind of response, one of the soldiers pulled his rifle off his back and brought the butt of his weapon down hard on Richardson's temple. He went down without a word, the two pitchers tumbling down around him. The three horsemen turned their horses around and galloped off without a word, leaving the unconscious Richardson lying on the bridge behind them, the blood from his skull spreading into the pool of spilt ale under him.

The townsfolk in the tavern noticed that their host was missing a few hours later and went in search of him. They found Richardson on the bridge shortly after, bleeding heavily and pale as a ghost. Practically the entire town was gathered around his bedside when he died the next morning. His death was recognized as one of the greatest tragedies in Goose River's history; he was an ardent supporter of the Revolution who had lost so much during the fight for independence, only to be stricken down on the eve of victory. It was a tragedy too thick with irony simply to go down as another fatality. Over the years, the story of William Richardson was told again and again, becoming one of the more unfortunate folktales in the state of Maine.

Richardson's story, however, did not end on the bridge over Goose River with two empty pitchers of ale and a cracked skull. For not long after he was killed, residents of the Maine town began talking about inexplicable sightings of the deceased patriarch. They saw a shimmering image of him, slightly transparent, standing on the bridge, holding his two pitchers in the air with a broad smile on his face. He would stand there for a couple of moments before vanishing into the air. He looked so blissful, so utterly content, that witnesses shed tears of joy, thinking that he was coming back to let the people of Goose River know that he still shared in the joy of American independence.

But as the years passed people began to think twice about the transparent image of William Richardson. For not only did he continue to appear long after 1783, townsfolk also reported alarming run-ins with the deceased patriot. More than one Goose River resident had stories of bizarre experiences with the ghost. Rather than vanishing a few moments after he was spotted, the phantom of Richardson would remain visible long enough to walk up to onlookers and offer them a pitcher of ale. Sometimes he was even said to jump up onto carriages crossing Goose River Bridge, insisting that they have a sip of his brew before vanishing, pitchers and all, mere inches from frightened witnesses' faces.

In 1851, the settlement of Goose River had grown large enough to form its own municipality, and adopting the name of Rockport, separated from the municipality of Camden. By this time, all William Richardson's contemporaries had long since passed away, and few people could recall the day he was murdered. Nevertheless, his likeness continued to appear on Goose River Bridge, standing in his absurd stance, with his wide grin and two pitchers held in perpetual offering. By this time, Richardson's identity had faded from the public memory and the image was dubbed "the Pitcher Man" by local storytellers who told the tragic tale of a man who was killed when all he wanted was to share a drink.

The Pitcher Man has continued to linger on Goose River Bridge to this very day. It seems as if the proliferation of automobiles has done nothing to kill his enthusiasm for a drink. Rockport motorists have seen him in broad daylight, standing in 18th-century dress, presenting his two full jugs to bewildered onlookers. Descriptions of these sightings have varied from witness to witness.

Those who have encountered Richardson on foot often claim to have felt quite troubled by the Pitcher Man.

Although he approaches with a broad grin, there is something extremely sad about him—as if he's holding back tears of agony through an artificial smile. For some, the Pitcher Man has vanished before they were able to get a close look, while others state that they've been followed across the bridge by the smiling apparition, which disappears only when it is about to step off the overpass.

And then there are the accounts of those driving across the Goose River Bridge in their vehicles. The Pitcher Man is much more determined to get the attention of motorists than pedestrians. While many people in their cars have had the good fortune of observing the Pitcher Man through the windshields of their cars, others have had far more startling experiences. On occasion, the Pitcher Man has shown more than the usual determination to share his ale, jumping through open car windows in an attempt to share his beer. Reactions have differed, often depending how long Richardson remains in the car. Sometimes he remains on the passenger side for long moments. On other occasions, he vanishes the moment he gets in the car, leaving drivers wondering about their own perceptions.

It is not known why the details of William Richardson sightings differ so much from witness to witness. Why does he seem more enthusiastic about getting ale to some people and less eager with others? Why do some motorists only spot him for a moment before he vanishes, while others witness him barreling into their vehicles? Indeed, the only thing that remains consistent about the Pitcher Man's behavior is his curious silence. All the figure ever does is beam at observers and hoist his two ale jugs into the air. Obviously bereft of the power of speech, the

Pitcher Man either lacks the organs to express himself verbally or is too inebriated to speak. It is impossible to say which is true.

Whatever the case, no one has ever dared to sip the Pitcher Man's ale. Maybe this is what Richardson is waiting for: someone to take a swig of the brew that he's offering. God knows he paid a high enough price for trying to share it over 200 years ago. In this light, maybe his repeated attempts at getting people to try his ale is his way of convincing himself that he died for a worthwhile cause. Certainly a man with the lofty worldly ambitions of William Richardson would need some way of coping with the tragic conditions of his demise.

4
Historic Thoroughfares

Roads and highways exist solely for automobile traffic, but many of the spirits that reside on them pre-date cars. These ghosts appear on the asphalt modifications of thoroughfares that have been used for hundreds of years—passages that were made for other means of transportation. They are ghosts from a distant past that remind us that not all forms of transportation are powered by combustible fuels nor must everyone on the road travel towards a destination.

The Ghost of
Mad Anthony Wayne

He is one of Pennsylvania's favorite sons: General Anthony Wayne, the 18th-century Revolutionary War hero who gave over 20 of his 51 years in staunch service to the United States. He was both a fearless soldier whose heart thrilled in the chaos of battle and a careful general who never made command decisions without proper deliberation. But above all, Wayne was gifted with the amazing knack at pulling off major victories when the people of the fledgling United States most needed them. And while countless individuals threw their lives into building the young country, few could boast such stunning success at repulsing America's enemies as could the Pennsylvania-born general.

The name Anthony Wayne probably doesn't figure largely in the lives of most Pennsylvanians today, yet the general's legacy is apparent on any map of the state. In addition to the municipalities of Wayne, Waynesboro and Waynesburg, nine townships and one county bear his namesake. For those of us who choose not to believe in an afterlife, such widespread recognition may well be regarded as getting as close to immortality as an individual can get.

According to the following tale, however, a person can achieve an entirely different sort of immortality, regardless of place names and legendary acclaim. Besides contributing his name to various locales in Pennsylvania, Anthony Wayne has left his very remains spread across the state. Some of the general is respectfully buried in the

The ghost of American patriot "Mad" Anthony Wayne is said to ride a phantom steed.

state's northwest corner, in Presque Isle, Erie, while other remains rest quietly in the southeast corner, in the small hamlet of Radnor, Chester County. The rest of him is scattered anywhere between. Those of us who are inclined to consider the afterlife a real possibility might be able to see how such a bizarre state of postmortem affairs—in addition to an untimely death at the peak of his career—

might impel the spirit of Anthony Wayne to haunt the state that bred him.

Wayne was born in Radnor on January 1, 1745. Not much about his early life suggested he was bound to achieve the status of living—and later on, not-so-living—legend. The only thing that really stood out about the young Wayne was his fervent love for all matters military. A mediocre student, he owed most of his opportunities to the favors of patronage and his family's lofty social standing. After a failed attempt at land surveying in his early twenties, he returned to Radnor to work with his father, helping on the family farm.

Wayne was 30 years old when his father died, leaving the young man with considerable wealth at his disposal. His inherited affluence made him one of Chester County's leading men, and when the exigencies of the American Revolution rolled through Pennsylvania, Anthony Wayne became the representative of his county, fearlessly taking up the sword against British tyranny. No one had to twist his arm.

Anthony Wayne had fantasized about military glory during his younger years. When it became clear to him that the political unrest of the day would provide an opportunity to live out his dreams of battle, he jumped into the fray. Enthusiasm and influence were enough to make a man officer material in the Continental Army, and by January 3, 1776, Wayne was commissioned as colonel of the Fourth Pennsylvania Battalion. It was the start of a long and illustrious military career.

He distinguished himself as one of the Revolutionary War's preeminent military figures, able to mold any group of men under his command into a premier fighting force. Wayne was cautious with his strategies, but when the time came for a fight the dauntless general could be found among the front lines of his men, roaring in the face of the enemy. It was this tendency to revel in the physical dangers of battle that earned him the sobriquet "Mad" Anthony Wayne, one of the more illustrious names to go down in the annals of American history.

On his first battle command, Wayne's battalion covered the retreat of the American army out of Canada after the Battle of Three Rivers. Promoted to brigadier general following his command of Fort Ticonderoga, Wayne led his troops at Brandywine Creek, where he held back the British Army while Washington and his defeated force retreated to safety. Remaining in the thick of the action throughout the rest of the war, Anthony Wayne was already one of the colonials' more famous officers when he won his famous victory at Stony Point.

The legendary attack took place on July 16, 1779. On the evening of that day, Wayne personally led a bayonet attack on the British fort. The general was grazed by a bullet during the approach and had to be carried over the parapet by his men, but he remained in command of his unit until the battle was over, bellowing orders over the clash of combat as the American soldiers captured the fort's flag and took more than 500 British prisoners. Stony Point was a major morale boost for the revolutionaries, who had won too few military victories against the British Army. Fighting the British later on in Virginia and in Georgia, Mad Anthony Wayne survived the Revolutionary War and became a hero. After the colonies had won their independence, he returned into civilian life.

But just as it was before the war, Mad Anthony wasn't as proficient at civilian life as he was at military service. Indeed, after a failed attempt at running a plantation in Georgia and a number of botched political ambitions, Mad Anthony considered himself lucky that there was still enough trouble on the continent to require a man of his abilities. Hostile Indians and a persistent British presence west of the Ohio River impelled George Washington to create a standing American army. Anthony Wayne was chosen to be commander-in-chief of the country's first army.

On August 20, 1794, Anthony Wayne led the Legion of the United States to a resounding victory at the Battle of Fallen Timbers, defeating the war chief Little Turtle and the Miami Confederacy that had assembled under him. The resulting Treaty of Greenville effectively brought peace, suppressing the alliance of Indians in the region. Without the presence of hostile Indians to stem the surging tide of American settlers, the British could not support their own presence in the forts around the Great Lakes. They were consequently forced to abandon those outposts and with them any last hopes that they would dominate affairs on the continent.

Like a victorious Caesar returning from Gaul, Mad Anthony Wayne was at the peak of his career when he traveled back to Pennsylvania in the winter of 1796. With his recently won laurels, we can only guess what sort of future was ahead of him. Some historians claim that his popularity was such that even the presidency was within his reach. Of this we can never be certain. On his way back to Pittsburgh, he became ill and was forced to remain in Erie. He would never beat the illness. Whatever ambitions he entertained died with him along the shores of Lake Erie. He passed away in a newly constructed blockhouse and was given a soldier's burial under the flagpole. So passed one of America's greatest.

But his story does not end there. Thirteen years later, Wayne's son Isaac made the trip from Chester County up to Erie to take his father's remains back to the family plot in Radnor. Those involved in the grisly work of exhuming the general's corpse must have been shocked and dismayed when they discovered that his body was remarkably well preserved. Isaac, understandably unwilling to transport the rotting corpse of his father across the state in the back of his wagon, consulted a doctor for advice. It was decided that the best course of action would be to boil what was once Mad Anthony Wayne in a caldron, thus separating the dead general's bones from his tissue.

Those fleshy remains of Mad Anthony Wayne that were left in the bottom of the pot after his skeleton was removed were once again buried in Erie. Today the blockhouse remains standing as a memorial to the first president's greatest war captain.

Wayne's bones, however, were not so fortunate. Roads in the early 19th century were completely different than they are today, and as Isaac made his way down what is now US Route 322, the wagon lifted and swung over the rocky, heavily rutted road. Legend has it that a good number of Mad Anthony Wayne's bones were jolted from the wagon on the long road, creating a rough trail of the general's bones from Erie to Radnor. After a ceremony in St.

Some of General Wayne's remains were buried in Radnor,
Pennsylvania, while the rest were mistakenly scattered elsewhere.

David's Church in Radnor on July 4, 1809, what was left
of Wayne's skeleton was buried in the family plot.

Yet according to countless eyewitnesses, his rest has
not been peaceful. In fact, on every New Year's Day since
he was buried, an apparition of the dead general has been

spotted along Route 322, tearing down the highway on his horse at a terrible speed, passing straight through anything in his way. Some eyewitnesses have even seen the details of his uniform—the epaulets on his shoulders, his saber bouncing on his side and his tricorne hat sitting atop his powdered wig.

These people have reported that his blank eyes dart from one side of the road to the other, as if in search of something that is lying along the side of the highway. Such accounts give credence to the popular theory that Mad Anthony's ghost is looking for missing bones that were not buried in Radnor. According to this belief, the apparition is Anthony Wayne's supernatural expression of his discontent at having his remains disturbed and strewn across the state.

There are other theories as well. A few of Wayne's biographers write about how difficult it must have been for the headstrong general to face such a meek end on his deathbed so soon after winning glory on the battlefield. If Mad Anthony Wayne had had his druthers, he would have surely preferred to fall in a hail of musket fire than in the quiet comfort of an Erie blockhouse. And surely his last breaths must have brought with them the realization that if his frail mortal frame was not failing him, his victory at Fallen Timbers may have cast him into the highest echelons of society. The world was finally his oyster, but he could not even get out of bed. Those who shudder at the thought of such frustrated ambitions are more inclined to believe that Mad Anthony's apparition has more to do with the general's anger at never being able to enjoy the fruits of his labors.

Either way, any drivers taking US Route 322 on New Year's Day best beware. Unless they don't mind having a 200-year-old ghost pass straight through their car, it would be wise to give any ghostly horseman in the rearview mirror the right of way.

A Slave's Vengeance

Old Squire was on his deathbed. He lay on a crude straw mattress in the slaves' quarters, surrounded by almost every slave that worked with him on the North Carolina plantation. His breathing came in short, painful rasps, punctuated by vicious coughing fits that yielded mouthfuls of bloody tissue. Gripped by a virulent fever, he stared in wide-eyed terror at some horrible hallucination that the people standing around his bed could only guess at. "It serves you right," he muttered at his personal demon, unseen to everyone present. "You never did anybody any bit of good, and now you're paying for it, evil man."

All the slaves packed into the late Master Lynch's slave quarters looked anxiously at the beloved man who lay dying before them. Old Squire had been a good and gentle man to every one of those dispossessed souls who had come into service at the Lynch plantation. He took care of the young and counseled the old; he shouldered more than his share of the labor and protected recalcitrant slaves from the ire of their frightful master. He was the heart of the congregation of black men and women who had the misfortune of being branded by Master Lynch. And he was dying.

Many attribute a tragic slave story to the strange sights and sounds at Mill Creek Bridge in North Carolina.

No one really knew what he was dying of, but there was much whispering about the nature of Old Squire's illness, which he contracted soon after Master Lynch had gone missing. Those who had been tending to the elderly black man since he had fallen ill heard him muttering strained words into the air, staring up at empty space with fear and defiance in his eyes. None of the slaves had seen anything like the sickness Old Squire was afflicted with, and it wasn't long before the slaves were convinced that their kind patriarch was being tortured by the rotten soul of their missing master. There was no small measure of wishful thinking in such a theory. For when word spread that Master Lynch had vanished two months previous, there wasn't a single slave on the plantation who did not secretly wish the worst on the cruel slave driver. If Lynch truly had passed on and was haunting Old Squire, at least he wouldn't be able to torture them any longer.

Old Squire wasn't the only one who was haunted by Master Lynch's sudden disappearance early in May 1820. Soon after Lynch had gone missing, people around Smithfield, North Carolina, began to experience strange things on Mill Creek Bridge, just south of town. Terror-stricken men would come galloping into Smithfield late at night, babbling hysterically about being attacked by an invisible man as they rode across the bridge. Horses reacted to the crossing as if they were being urged to walk off the edge of a cliff, and many an unsuspecting rider was suddenly thrown from his mount when his horse came to a sudden stop just before the creek. Numerous travelers crossing the bridge at night claimed that the torches they carried would inexplicably go out the moment they stepped on the bridge, only to reignite the instant they were on the opposite bank.

Others reported hearing strange sounds coming from the woods when they stepped on Mill Creek Bridge. Whether in broad daylight or in the middle of the night, travelers often heard the sound of a whip cracking along the edge of the creek. There were also some who said they heard Master Lynch's voice barking orders at someone in the woods just beyond the bridge. But anyone who followed the missing man's voice always stumbled on the same deserted, partially cleared, forest.

Rumors quickly spread through the community. Many townsfolk in Smithfield suspected that the missing slave owner was responsible for the bizarre happenings on Mill Creek Bridge. Lynch had never been a well-liked man; cruel, filthy and vicious, he despised everyone who walked on two legs. He was the town pariah, a man who was considered perverse enough by locals that few had any difficulty imagining him stalking travelers crossing Mill Creek Bridge.

The slaves at Lynch's plantation also believed that their former master was lurking around Mill Creek Bridge, but they had reason to believe that there were much more sinister forces at work on the muggy land around the creek. For the last time any of them had seen Master Lynch he was heading to the bridge with the intention of clearing the land there. Old Squire accompanied him. Morning turned to noon, which gave way to midday, but there was no sign of either slave or master. Even when the sun began sinking into the horizon, there was still no trace of Master Lynch or Old Squire. The slaves began to worry about their elderly patriarch. Most had been on the wrong end of Master Lynch's cruelty at one time or another, and they began to fear the worst for gentle Old Squire.

Everyone was surprised, then, when Old Squire stumbled into the slaves' quarters late that evening. He looked more dead than alive, with barely enough strength to stay on his feet. Thick layers of mud caked his legs, arms and hands, which were also smeared with dark splotches of blood. But it was the look in Old Squire's eyes that every-one remembered. The other slaves had always drawn comfort from the warm glow that radiated from Old Squire's compassionate eyes; now they were twin orbs of vacuous horror. He stood at the doorway for an instant, staring blankly at the building's shocked inhabitants before collapsing unconscious in front of them.

Years of cruel servitude under Master Lynch conveyed a certain stoicism on the slaves. Without a word, they picked Old Squire off the ground, washed him up and put him to bed, hoping that time would heal whatever wounds Lynch had inflicted. It soon became obvious, however, that more had transpired on that summer day than they had initially believed. They had assumed that Old Squire was worked past the point of endurance and then encouraged to work some more by the end of a whip. In the past, Master Lynch had shown no qualms about working his slaves to death. But none of them guessed that the wound Old Squire had received ran much deeper than the whip marks that cut across his back.

The slaves instantly grew suspicious when Master Lynch didn't show up the next day to oversee their labor. Lynch was quite a diligent man when it came to ensuring that his captive workforce was doing its job, so the slaves knew something was amiss when Lynch was absent again the day after. A week later, Lynch was declared missing throughout Johnston County. All the while, Old Squire was convulsing under an inexplicable fever, wailing through frightful hallucinations, calling out the name of his master. Some of the things that he said caused his caretakers great concern. He yelled threats at an unseen

Master Lynch, hollering that he would kill the man if he was whipped one more time. And then he implored an invisible presence for a brief rest, for only a small sip of water. These requests obviously fell on deaf ears, for they were often followed by a long piteous howl at the ceiling.

And so although most people in Johnston County believed that Master Lynch had taken to terrorizing travelers crossing Mill Creek Bridge, Lynch's slaves had darker suspicions. Many were convinced that a violent altercation had taken place when the two men had gone to work by the bridge—a confrontation that had ended with Lynch's murder. It was Lynch's dark soul, they believed, that was tormenting those who crossed Mill Creek and causing Old Squire's hallucinations. The following years gave credence to the slaves' interpretation of the events near Smithfield.

Old Squire's condition worsened throughout the summer, and by mid-July he was sucking in his last breaths through tortured rasps. But just before he gave up the ghost, he made a dramatic confession. Old Squire' words spread like wildfire through the plantation and have been repeated countless times over the years, passed on orally from one generation to the next, so that it is impossible to know what his exact words were. Yet the different versions of Old Squire's last words differ only slightly.

"You knew him as well as I," Old Squire gasped to the slaves standing around his bed. "He was a terrible man, without love for no one or nothing but himself. We all bore him the best we could, but in the end I was the weak one. I was the sinner who struck him down once and for all. Me and him were workin' out by Mill Creek Bridge. For some reason, Lynch got it in that muddled head of his to clear out that worthless swampland, and he was gonna kill me doin' it. I broke my back for the entire day, not allowed to even *look* at water, let alone drink. If I let up even for a second, Lynch put the whip to me. Well, the heat, the thirst, the whip and his cruelty put the Devil in me, and the next time he raised his whip that hoe jumped from my hands all by itself. I hit him hard across the face, and when he fell into the mud, I kept at him—I kept at him until he was dead. It was me. I killed that devil of a man that day and, God help me, I would do it again if I had the chance. He's buried in the mud under the Mill Creek Bridge."

Old Squire interrupted his confession when his eyes fell on something unseen hovering behind the heads of his listeners. "Do you hear me?" he hollered at whatever floated near the ceiling. "I'd strike you down again, you godless demon, and none of your howlin' or grinnin' would change that! You're dead and buried, so go back to the dirt I put you in." Although he looked defiant, it was obvious the exchange with the invisible Lynch had taken a lot out of him.

"But death hasn't kept that devil from me. He hasn't wandered far from my side since I buried him. He's been here ever since, grinning at me from the corners of this cursed room, waiting for me to join him in the afterworld."

Hours after his confession, Old Squire finally passed away. The slaves decided to keep Old Squire's dying words to themselves, and for the next few years the story of Lynch's demise was kept from the community. Meanwhile, strange things continued to occur on the bridge.

Travelers continued to be attacked by invisible assailants, horses continued to balk at crossing the creek and strange noises still emerged from the swamp around the bridge. Eventually, locals began questioning the validity of their suspicions regarding the missing Master Lynch. To keep up these pranks for months was one thing, but it would take a morbid determination that no madman possessed to continue harassing commuters on the Mill Creek Bridge for so many years. And some of the phenomena that occurred were far too strange to be the work of the living.

One man who was walking across the bridge in the evening felt an invisible force pull his cane upward from his hand and into the night sky. When he reached the other end of the bridge, the cane gently dropped from the darkness above back into his hand. Over the years, the sounds of struggle in the surrounding bushes began to fade, replaced by an unearthly wailing coming from underneath the bridge. Numerous other people approaching the bridge reported seeing lights flashing over the bridge late in the evening, only to find nothing there by the time they reached the bridge. It was then that the citizens living around Smithfield began to suspect that something inhuman was lurking around the bridge.

No one knows exactly how Old Squire's story spread beyond his confidants, but the account of the slave driver's murder eventually circulated throughout the county. Some tried to dig up Lynch's remains, hoping to give the man a proper burial, but his corpse was never found. It has been suggested that the saturated earth around the creek may have caused his body to decompose quickly. Others believe that the first slaves who heard about the murder may have dug up Lynch and hidden his body to avoid the ire of racist whites. And then there were those who said that Old Squire's deathbed confession was a delirious dream, mistaken for reality in the last feverish moments of his life, and that he had not killed Master Lynch after all. These skeptics concluded that the strange goings on at the bridge were a combination of natural phenomena and tall tales.

Nevertheless, accounts of strange events on the bridge have persisted over the years. To this day, motorists driving down Shaw's Creek Road off Highway 701 have continued to report strange sights and sounds on Mill Creek Bridge, where the surrounding swamp still seems to impose an intangible malice on all who cross.

The Ghost of Queen Boadicea

She is seen late at night on the B1398 Road, near Cammeringham in the county of Lincolnshire, England. It is always on a foggy moonless night in the fall, when the damp chill of the coming winter rolls in off the North Sea. The sound is the first indication of her approach: thundering hooves clattering upon the road, the rumble of wheels rolling heavily on the road and a woman's strong voice rising above the clamor. No one has been able to place what language she speaks. It seems like some variation of a Celtic tongue, but the sound of her approach is always too loud to make out exactly what she is saying— only that her voice is high and terrible and strong.

And then, in the span of a single moment, she is there, looming over the hapless witness, standing atop an

Engraving of Queen Boadicea, the Celtic ruler whose appearances atop a phantom chariot continue to terrify Lincolnshire residents.

enormous chariot. Her two snorting horses, one white as bone, the other black as coal, move impossibly fast, leaving a trail of curling fog behind them. The woman herself is a picture of statuesque beauty, standing over six feet tall, wild and terrifying. She is dressed in loose, flowing robes with long red hair blowing wildly around her. When her unfortunate victims are on foot, she stares down at them imperiously, wagging a long finger and screaming out some long and unintelligible threat. Those who have spotted her while driving their cars have only had a chance to swerve out of the way in a panicked rush as she tears by, hell-bent on getting to some unknown destination. And then she is gone, as quickly as she came.

Everyone knows her as Queen Boadicea, a Celtic ruler whose short, violent reign over the Iceni ended in the defeat of her people. It all happened nearly 2000 years ago. The area that is now Norfolk, England, was cast into savage warfare, where the Iceni were locked in a bloody struggle with the invading Romans. Boadicea was married to King Prasutagus, a prosperous monarch whose reign over the Iceni had lasted for quite some time.

When the Romans invaded in 43 AD, Prasutagus kept his throne by accepting his status as a client king to the invading power. The Iceni stayed at peace with the Romans for almost two decades, until Prasutagus finally succumbed to old age. The conditions of inheritance that the Iceni king willed before he died enacted the chain of events that would lead to Boadicea's historical uprising.

Prasutagus believed he had devised a satisfactory solution concerning his heir. Recognizing his obligations to the Roman Empire, he ordered that half his holdings go to the Roman Emperor, while his wife, Queen Boadicea, would inherit the other half of Iceni. Perhaps Prasutagus believed that the two parties would be able to share power over the region, and this concession to the empire would ensure that Rome would look kindly on the Iceni. He was greatly mistaken.

Not only did the Romans expect to inherit the entire kingdom, but governors of the strictly patriarchal society were also deeply offended that Prasutagus assumed that Romans would share power with a provincial queen. The Roman military went to work. Soon after Prasutagus' death, around 59 AD, centurions set their legionaries loose on the Iceni. Homes were plundered, the late king's relatives lost their lands and were put into slavery, the king's two daughters were tortured and Boadicea herself was publicly flogged. The Romans believed that this severe retaliation would subdue the Iceni, but in this they too were greatly mistaken.

Queen Boadicea was bent on vengeance. Mounting a chariot with her two daughters, she rode through every corner of her kingdom, summoning everyone old enough to carry a weapon. Poems have been written about the marshalling of the Iceni, during which the legendary Briton formed one of the largest Celtic armies the Romans had ever seen. They wreaked havoc on the Roman colony of Britannia, sacking and plundering every village they came across in southern Briton, even putting the colony capital, Londinium—now London—to the sword.

Queen Boadicea's Britons continued on this path of destruction until they met Suetonius Paulinus' army on the field of battle near present-day West Midlands. Although the Roman governor's army was vastly outnumbered, it was in full possession of the historical Roman discipline. After a vicious battle, the Romans brought total defeat to Boadicea's army, crushing the rebellion once and for all. Boadicea herself fled the battlefield, committing suicide soon afterwards by ingesting a lethal dose of poison.

Reestablishing their control over the recalcitrant colony, the Romans would remain overlords of Britain for the next four centuries. Boadicea's short-lived insurrection faded into the historical memory, a footnote in the century-long account of the United Kingdom.

Although the long-term significance of Boadicea's uprising was generally reduced to historical irrelevance, her spirit somehow survived in the national mythology of Britain. Boadicea enjoyed rejuvenated popularity in the 19th century, when many European nations looked to the past for historical icons with admirable national traits. It was then that the story of Boadicea received renewed attention. Hailed as a hero of the British people, she stood for rebellion against an invading power. In 1902, a statue of the long-dead queen was erected near the British Houses of Parliament. Standing upon a chariot pulled by two rearing horses, Boadicea is depicted in a pose of noble defiance, calling upon her people to rise up with two upraised arms. She stares stoically into the distance, as if in full knowledge of her eventual fate, but committed to action nevertheless. Inspired, British Poet Laureate Lord Alfred Tennyson wrote a poem about the Iceni queen's terrible uprising.

While many have questioned the practice of rewriting histories to advance contemporary political agendas, scores of nocturnal sightings on the B1398 Road in Lincolnshire have added to Boadicea's legend. Those few commuters who have been treated to the sight of the ageless queen thundering down the road on her chariot come away from the experience with a new appreciation for her story.

Some witnesses have commented on her beauty, others on the expression of rage so clearly visible on her face. And then there are those who claim they nearly crashed their vehicles trying to evade the speeding vehicle, invariably described as moving far too fast, even for two horses at a full gallop. No one knows exactly who was the first to see Boadicea racing through her former realm, but the stories of the phantom chariot go back more than a century, when travelers were nearly thrown off their startled horses when the queen came tearing out of the foggy darkness. There were also numerous reports of overturned wagons along B1398, their passengers hurt and their drivers stunned into a fearful silence.

We can only guess why the spirit of Boadicea continues to materialize. Some claim that she began appearing in the 1880s, when the British Empire began to fall into gradual decline. This theory has Boadicea appearing to warn the British of the impending end of empire. Others believe that Boadicea is merely reliving those instances in her life that were too traumatic for her spirit to forget, even after death. These people claim that she has been going on nightly rides ever since she was killed. They maintain that the many sightings of her in Lincolnshire in the last century relate to population increases in the country. At the same time, the general erosion of traditional religious values in the countryside has allowed locals to feel more comfortable in talking about such matters. Then there are those who claim that the public attention lavished on the long-forgotten queen in the late 19th century brought her spirit back from the dead. Could it be that the Iceni queen felt obliged to start appearing before a people who were suddenly revering her?

Whatever the case, reports of Boadicea along the B1398 Road persist today. Travelers are urged to be cautious if they are on the road at night and a thick fog starts to roll in off the North Sea. Queen Boadicea and her horse-drawn chariot might be waiting around the very next bend.

The Ghosts of the Bloody Pit

The Hoosac Tunnel is one of America's great forgotten feats. A five-mile railroad tunnel burrowing into the Berkshire Mountains of northwest Massachusetts, the structure stands as one of the most incredible engineering accomplishments of the 19th century. Construction began in 1851, and by the time it was completed in 1874, it was the longest transportation tunnel in America, second in the world only to the Mont Cenis railroad tunnel on the French–Italian border.

But the passage through the Berkshires was paid for dearly. Built early during the United States' industrial development, the path was dug out of the mountain with every kind of tool ever used to blast rock out of the way. Workers used their hands, gunpowder, new machines and nitroglycerine. Some techniques worked and others didn't, but what made the Hoosac such a historical event was that they learned something new with every new method and technology employed. The hole they were digging under the Berkshires was a pioneer effort that would set the standard for all the other tunnels dug in North America. Nevertheless, it proved to be a costly process, claiming the lives of 196 men in the 24 years it took to finish.

Most accounts of the tunnel's construction focus on the incredible accomplishment of the tunnel itself and

Many workers died during the construction of the Hoosac Tunnel—a likely cause of its notorious haunting.

the measures that were taken to complete it, relegating the fatalities to unpleasant historical footnotes. Yet many believe the casualties of the Hoosac serve as reminders of the demanding and dangerous work that was required to construct it. Indeed, it is the human cost of the tunnel's construction that stands out today, when people have difficulty wrestling with the idea of such a lethal workplace.

One man died for every 127 feet that was dug into the mountain—which makes the Hoosac much more than a railroad passage through the Berkshires. Individuals only need glance at either the eastern or western entrances of the tunnel to get a sense of the foreboding darkness blanketing the tracks. It could be described as the same feeling one gets while visiting a cemetery or a battlefield—the inexplicable gravity one feels around the sites of great tragedies.

So while the industrial accomplishment of Hoosac Tunnel is lauded in the history books, the tunnel's industrial tomb is often perceived in the same light as a historic cemetery or famous battlefield. And just as these celebrated monuments to the dead are often occupied by denizens of the underworld, so too does the Hoosac Tunnel boast its share of ghosts. Bizarre occurrences were reported as early as 1866, when the tunnel was still being built, and the legends of ghosts in the mountain continue today, kept alive by paranormal investigators and curiosity seekers who have witnessed paranormal activity in the tunnel's darkness.

The most famous ghost story involves three explosives experts named Ned Brinkman, Billy Nash and Ringo Kelley, who were working on the tunnel in 1865. Calling these men "experts" is a bit of an exaggeration. The fact is, no one in 1865 could call himself an expert with nitro-glycerine. The highly volatile liquid explosive had just been introduced as an industrial agent, and few felt confident or comfortable using it. It was used to clear away rock in lieu of gunpowder for the first time in the Hoosac Tunnel, and it is said that most of the workers who had been killed while the tunnel was being built were casualties of the unstable and lethal new substance.

The details of the Brinkman, Nash and Kelley tragedy are shrouded in mystery. What is certain is that Ned Brinkman and Billy Nash were planting nitroglycerine against the tunnel wall on March 20, 1865, when Ringo Kelley prematurely set off the charge. Both Brinkman and Nash were killed in the ensuing blast; Kelley emerged from the rubble without a scratch. The circumstances behind the deaths were questionable enough to cast suspicion on Kelley. He quit his job in the Hoosac Tunnel shortly after the incident and vanished completely for a year. It is said that no one—neither friends nor family— ever saw him alive again. Of course, Kelley's sudden disappearance only stoked workers' suspicion more, and in his absence practically everyone working the Hoosac concluded that foul play was involved in the deaths of Brinkman and Nash.

Just over a year after the tragedy, on March 30, 1866, Ringo Kelley reappeared. His dead body was found about two miles into the tunnel, on the exact same spot where Brinkman and Nash were killed a year before. A look of extreme terror was frozen onto Kelley's bone-white face and ugly bruises covered his throat. It was determined that someone or something of incredible strength had strangled Kelley to death.

The discovery of Kelley's corpse sent shudders through the demoralized workforce laboring under the Berkshires. Contrary to common sense, many of the men suspected that Kelley was killed by the vengeful ghosts of Brinkman and Nash. It was around this time that the legend of the Hoosac Tunnel was born. Believing that they were boring a cursed tunnel, miners began whispering about strange sights and sounds coming from the darkness while they worked. Men who were willing to take their chances with gunpowder and nitroglycerine quit their jobs when confronted with the prospect of supernatural forces.

Accounts of strange phenomena continued over the subsequent months. Spine-tingling moans regularly drifted through the dank tunnel as workers sweated in the darkness. Some swore they heard groans of pain coming from nowhere, as if the walls themselves were protesting the intrusion of rock picks and explosives. In the fall of 1868, the construction company hired a detective to investigate the sounds. If company officials expected the detective, Paul Travers, a respected mechanical engineer and former officer in the Civil War, to allay workers' fears with a rational report, they were sorely disappointed. After one month of investigation, Travers proclaimed that he had been frightened more than once during his time in the Hoosac Tunnel, and he could offer no explanation for the strange noises that he himself had heard underneath the Berkshires.

One month later, another disaster struck. A gas explosion on the surface sent hot debris tearing through the tunnel, turning the incomplete Hoosac into a hellhole. Dead men were heaped in the darkness within, while the cries of the wounded could be heard through the entire work site. The workers cleared the tunnel of the casualties and debris as quickly as they could, but the dead, and parts of the dead, continued to show up throughout the following year.

This event only added to the legend that was growing around the tunnel. People from the nearby village began reporting strange occurrences around the Hoosac. All through the winter of 1868–69 there were strange sightings near the tunnel entrance and in the surrounding forests. Semi-transparent images of miners were seen all over the mountain. Some said these men looked forlorn, slouched low with pickaxes or shovels slung over their drooping shoulders, wandering aimlessly as if lost in the alpine foliage, leaving not a trace of their passing in the snow or the bush. In other sightings enraged miners with horrendous wounds appeared out of nowhere to rush at terrified witnesses, filling them with dread rather than pity. In the span of an instant, onlookers went from expecting an attack to standing alone in the snow. These occurrences repeated themselves with such frequency during the winter that the ghosts of Hoosac Tunnel were instantly enshrined in the canon of local folklore.

The Hoosac Tunnel was renamed "the bloody pit" by local storytellers with a penchant for dramatization, and its legend grew with every death that occurred thereafter. By the time the tunnel was completed, the experimental application of nitroglycerine had claimed so many lives that the Hoosac deserved its gruesome moniker.

The tales are manifold. Intermittent moaning, wails and shouts of warning that were heard on and off by workers while the tunnel was being constructed; these continued long after the miners finished their work. Engineers often heard horrendous screams echoing off the tunnel's walls over the roaring of their trains' engines. Hunters, hikers and adventurers venturing near the Hoosac's entrance claimed to hear similar cries spilling from the darkness of the tunnel. Most who had these experiences tended to get away from the tunnel as quickly as their legs could take them, but some were drawn to the eerie noises coming from within and ventured in to take a look.

Two such men were Greg Jefferies and Ian Bolt, who were hunting near the Hoosac Tunnel in the fall of 1874. Legend has it that the young men were drawn to the tunnel entrance by the sound of a man moaning in agony. Both Jefferies and Bolt knew about the tunnel's haunted reputation and were suddenly thrilled at the idea of confronting one of the ghosts in the Hoosac.

Wide-eyed and buzzing with nervous energy, the two friends walked tentatively into the tunnel. One held a lantern aloft; the other tightly clutched his rifle. The painful groans grew louder as the two men walked further into the darkness, eventually becoming so clear that the pair began to imagine that a grievously wounded man might indeed be lying within the tunnel.

As the minutes past, Bolt became more and more convinced of the possibility that a living man lay just beyond the lantern's light. "Hello!" Bolt called out into the darkness. "Are you badly hurt?"

As soon as the words were out of his mouth, the moans stopped. "I said hello there!" Bolt called again. "Tell us where you are so that we can help." The ensuing seconds brought a heavy silence—the only sound in the black tunnel was the autumn wind blowing over the trees outside, whistling along the railroad tracks that reached under the mountain. That was when Bolt and Jefferies heard the sound of slow, heavy footsteps approaching from out of the darkness.

Bolt hoisted his dim lantern a little higher over his head and squinted into the black, but couldn't see a thing. A faint chill began to creep down both men's necks. The idea of turning around and leaving occurred to them, but the tortured moans that had filled the tunnel a few minutes earlier came back to them. They remained standing there. Jefferies' hands tightened around his rifle when Bolt called out again. "Just lay still, and we'll come to you."

In the next instant, a light suddenly appeared within the mountain. It was a faint point of light, swaying gently as it slowly moved towards them, along with the footsteps that continued on their plodding path. "It's a man with a lantern, he's probably working here," Jefferies whispered to his friend, trying to ignore the agonized wails that had just recently filled the tunnel. "What do you want to do?"

"Let's go see what his problem is," Bolt said. "He might need help."

With that, the two men cautiously began to move forward. The cold fear knotted in their backs grew with every step they took toward the approaching light. Bolt gave up calling to whoever was holding the lantern in front of them, and they went the rest of the way in silence until the mysterious individual was standing just beyond the light of Bolt's lantern. The next step brought them within eyeshot of the mysterious figure in the tunnel. What they saw there in the dim light of Hoosac Tunnel changed their lives forever.

He stood just over six feet tall. His miners' overalls were smudged with blood and dirt and a small lantern hung from his callused hand. He was standing still, having frozen when he got close enough to see Bolt and Jefferies. But something was wrong. Where the miner's head should have been was nothing but empty space. The moaning miner was headless.

The two men stopped to consider the plausibility of what stood in front of them before fleeing. Neither of them uttered a word to each other as they dashed through the tunnel. Nary a peep escaped their lips as they burst out into the crisp fall air. They kept running until the Hoosac was far behind them. It was then, nearly a half-hour later, that a breathless Jefferies turned to his friend and asked, "Did we really see what we saw?"

Countless others would ask a similar question as the pair's story spread through the county. While locals had become used to the strange stories about the tunnel, none had ever been this dramatic before, and there was some skepticism over what the pair had really seen in the tunnel that day. Was it was a product of their imaginations, a bald-faced lie or an actual ghost? Regardless of its nature, the account of the headless miner became one of the most often repeated Hoosac Tunnel tales. One tale among many.

If the sheer number of supernatural phenomena reported over the years is any indication, many of the 196 miners who lost their lives in the tunnel have remained behind to haunt it, although not all of them limit their activities to chasing away terrified witnesses.

More than one railroad worker claimed that his life was saved by sudden warnings shouted out from the darkness. Geoff Craig's life, for example, might have come to a premature end in 1972 if he hadn't listened to the urgent voice that commanded him to run. "I was inspecting the tracks about 80 yards into the tunnel when a shrill voice I never heard before began screaming at me. It was a man's voice, screaming 'Run! Run! Run!' over and over again. I ran without thinking, just as scared of the voice as I was of whatever danger it was warning me against."

Seconds after Craig started for the tunnel entrance, he heard the roar of an approaching train. One quick glance over his shoulder revealed the single headlight of a rapidly approaching locomotive. He made it out of the Hoosac Tunnel just as the train caught up with him, so close that he could feel the air rush by him when he dove out of its path. "I'll never know for certain who saved my life that day," Craig said later, "but I'm convinced it was one of those workers who died digging the tunnel so many years ago."

Could it be that some of the miners who lost their lives digging the Hoosac between 1851 and 1874 are reluctant to see any more lives lost in the tunnel? Geoff Craig isn't the only man who believes it. Thanks to the benevolent spirits under the mountain, other men have narrowly missed being electrocuted, disfigured or killed while working. Apparently, the idea of workers' solidarity still exists among the spirits of Hoosac Mountain.

Today, there are just as many frightening accounts of ghosts in the tunnel as ever. Why some ghosts terrorize witnesses while others behave magnanimously will probably remain a mystery. Perhaps the spirits are torn between anger at their own tragic deaths and a natural concern for their present-day counterparts. Or maybe it boils down to personality, since the dispositions of ghosts vary as much as the dispositions of living humans. Whatever the case, the ghosts of the Hoosac Tunnel continue to haunt the dark recesses under the Berkshires, both frightening and favoring those people who stumble across their paths.

The Yorkshire Highwaymen

"Peter Adler" lists a number of reasons he prefers to go by a pseudonym. "You know, it happened such a long time ago. It was 1969, and there have been many times since that night when I've thought about what I saw, and wondered if maybe I wasn't dreaming or hallucinating. Sometimes I wonder if that night ever even happened at all. Memory can be a deceptive thing when it's had entire decades to dwell on itself."

Adler continues to ponder what he saw that fall evening in northern England over 30 years ago because numerous others have reported similar experiences while traveling on the A640. The A640 Buckstones Road is an old path that snakes through the moorland of the Yorkshire Pennines. Hiking enthusiasts from all over the world have taken the A640 into the heart of some of Britain's most spectacular landscapes.

That is what drew Peter Adler of Massachusetts to the area in 1969. "I was a young man back then, barely 20 years old, and was in my second month of a five-month backpacking trip across Europe. I had just arrived in Yorkshire earlier that day and was really excited at the prospect of hiking through the Pennines." Young Adler was especially taken by the idea of seeing the moor by moonlight, so decided to spend his first night in Yorkshire walking along the country road.

"It was an incredible night," Adler remembers. "There was a full moon out and the highlands were lit up with this silver light. I'd never seen anything like it. Today, after all these years, the thing I remember most was the

An eyewitness had a startling encounter with some ghostly English highwaymen.

thrill of being there. I remember being really, really giddy, so far from home and walking through this incredible countryside by moonlight. That was just before *they* showed up."

Adler was walking across the moor, humming gladly at the night's sky, when the riders appeared in the distance— three men on horses, towing one riderless horse behind. "I wasn't sure what to make of them," Adler says. "Of course it struck me as strange that anybody would be out for a ride in the middle of the night, but what did I know? I was in a foreign country after all, so maybe this was some custom I didn't know about."

Things changed as the riders drew nearer. Something about the approaching horsemen suddenly struck Adler as sinister. "It was more than the strangeness of being out on a ride at that hour. Just the sight of them coming up the road over the desolate moor was suddenly terrifying. I can't recall exactly what was so frightening about them. It's just that they suddenly seemed somehow *unreal*—and the entire moor seemed to recognize it too. Everything suddenly got very, very still."

They drew nearer. It wasn't until the riders were about 50 yards away that Adler started to panic. "When they were close enough for me to see the details of their clothing and equipment, I realized then that there was something very wrong. These guys weren't your average Englishmen out on a late-night horseback ride. First off, they were dressed in outdated clothing…and when I say outdated, I mean *outdated*. They looked like they had stepped off the set of the *Last of the Mohicans* or something. Two of them had tricorne hats on, wore long coats with leather breeches and high riding boots. These men wore rapiers that hung low from sword belts, and were each armed with numerous pistols that jutted out of belts, jacket pockets and saddlebags. The third guy looked like he may have been their servant. His only weapon was a blunderbuss, which was latched to the saddle of his horse, and he was leading a packhorse that was heavily loaded with supplies."

While the riders' anachronistic clothing was strange enough, old fabric and outdated weapons alone weren't responsible for freezing Adler's feet to the ground in fear. "The air was getting colder and colder the closer these guys got. They were walking their horses slowly up the road, and I could hear their hooves clattering on the stone. By the time they were close enough for me to make out the whites of their eyes, the air was *freezing*. And these riders, they hadn't even acknowledged me; they just stared ahead with completely blank expressions. That was until they were right beside me. They were close enough for me to reach out and touch when one of them turned his head to face me. His head turned slowly on his neck, until he was looking right at me, or I should probably say, looking right *through* me, because that's what it felt like. It was like staring into the face of a moving statue."

His colorless eyes looked completely uninterested as he passed the petrified Adler, who was still frozen to the ground in horror. "I can't recall anything about his face anymore," Adler adds, "except for his eyes, which seemed about as human as the moonlight. I knew then that these weren't living men—that I was looking at the ghosts of three men who had died a long, long time ago."

When the rider slowly raised his hand and tipped his hat at Adler, something in the young man snapped. Death had nodded at him, and he felt the sudden urge to run. In the next instant he was tearing down the road as fast as his legs could carry him. He didn't make it far before he was breathless, the full backpack on his shoulders weighing him down. Suddenly seized by a fear that the riders had pursued him, Adler turned around to see how far back they were; not a soul was on the A640 behind him. The moor was still, quiet and deserted—moved only by a chill breeze that had picked up and was blowing across the highland.

Peter Adler found ways to forget his supernatural encounter on the Pennines over the years, but every now and then his thoughts would return to that moonlit night. Sometimes the memory seemed more like a dream than anything else, and most of the time he was content to think of it that way. But on other occasions, Adler says that the horseman's sightless gaze has come back to him as if it were yesterday. During those moments, he has felt an urgency to discover the identity of the three riders.

He has not been alone in this pursuit. Throughout the years, a number of people have seen the ghostly trio making their way down the A640 through the Pennines. Although the witnesses are usually in cars, not on foot, and seldom get as close to the horsemen as Peter Adler did, they always seem to spot the phantom riders around the same place, and always when a full moon is shining over the moor. Sometimes the motorists slow down enough to get a close look at the mysterious riders, while others, sensing the same intangible fear that Adler felt, drive past the horsemen as quickly as they can.

There has been much speculation over the identity of these horsemen. No one in the nearby villages of Uppermill or Denshaw has ever been suspected of going on these moonlit rides, and if any trio of young men were singled out for scaring nocturnal travelers on A640, they'd certainly be hard pressed to explain their disappearing act on the moor. The locals who have kept tabs on the riders over the years have come to accept that these equestrians are Yorkshire's resident ghosts—manifestations of three wayward souls who lost their lives many years ago.

The men's names will probably remain shrouded in the mists of history, but it has generally been accepted by all who have studied them that the trio was once a group of highwaymen—18th-century outlaws who made an iniquitous living on England's roads by robbing travelers of their money and valuables.

Why they continue to relive their ride through the Pennines is anyone's guess. Perhaps the modern-day A640 was the last route these robbers took before they were apprehended by the law. Maybe they were crossing the moor in haste, on the run from the authorities, and the fear they felt was so intense that some residue of it has remained behind long after the riders themselves passed away. Could it be that the apparitions are recurring manifestations of emotions that were felt nearly 300 years ago? Many believe so.

Whatever the case, the three mysterious highwaymen continue to appear on evenings when the moon is full, crossing the moor on the A640 in sullen silence, headed for a destination that witnesses can only guess at. They have been spotted by locals and tourists, motorists and hikers, policemen on patrol and midnight picnickers stealing quiet moments. All who have seen them report the same experiences: a marked drop in temperature as the riders approach, a sudden seizure of irrational fear and the silent, somber salute that one of the riders gives to the awestruck witness, slowly raising his hand to tip his hat at whoever is there to see him in the cold moonlight.

So it is not without warning that commuters should travel the A640 in Yorkshire when a full moon shines over the moor. If they are possessed by a fierce sensation of fear after they spot three riders in the distance, perhaps they should slow down and let the highwaymen pass. Fortunately, the men seem to have given up their earthly profession and have yet to empty anyone's pockets of pounds or pence.

Witch Duck Road

Grace Sherwood was always fiercely protective of her dignity. She lived the way she saw fit, and paid little attention to the whispered accusations, gossip and mockery that circulated through the Pungo area of Virginia Beach, Virginia. Grace was among the earliest settlers to arrive in North America, working to make a home for herself and her family when Virginia was a British colony and the American frontier did not extend any farther west than the Appalachian Mountains. Grace possessed the great strength and resourcefulness required to survive life in the New World.

Perhaps this strength of character caused her neighbors to dislike Grace. While most early Virginian women were expected to work alongside their men, Grace threw herself into the duties of homesteading a little too zealously for her contemporaries' liking. She was said to be a tall, strong and beautiful woman who could handle a greater workload than most of the men in Tidewater. She had opinions and had no qualms about expressing them as loudly as she wanted—which was usually a few decibels higher than what was acceptable. She wore men's pants, spit, swore and drank.

In the 17th century, non-conformity wasn't imbued with the same romance as it is today—especially among women. In fact, there were women in the United States and Europe who were being branded witches for their idiosyncrasies. Whether these ostracized women practiced witchcraft or were simply different from everyone else, the punishment for their activities was harsh, even fatal.

So Grace Sherwood and her husband, James, did not take it well when one of their neighbors, John Gisburne, accused Mrs. Sherwood of being a witch. Colonial court records reveal that Gisburne brought the charge against Grace in the summer of 1698. Gisburne was an unhappy old codger who was not having the best luck farming cotton. But when his hogs got sick after three consecutive years of bad crops, he became convinced that larger forces were conspiring against him. Evil forces.

Then, as now, most people believed that they could remedy their misfortunes. Few take powerlessness well. Someone, or something, has to be responsible for their troubles, and in John Gisburne's case, the scapegoat was Grace Sherwood. Economic desperation and 17th-century religious devotion made for a virulent combination in Gisburne. Taking all the local gossip about Grace to heart, he became convinced that his controversial neighbor's quirks amounted to something sinister.

He took to spying on the Sherwoods. During daylight hours, he crept through the bush on the Sherwood farm, keeping his eyes fixed on Grace as she went about her daily work, looking for anything unusual. At night, he would sneak up to the Sherwood cabin and peer into lit rooms, convinced that evil things were afoot. We can never know if Gisburne saw anything that confirmed his suspicions or was already certain before he began his investigation, but something in the man changed as he stalked Grace Sherwood. He soon felt comfortable enough making his private suspicions public.

Accusing Grace of witchcraft, Gisburne began spreading the word that she had been cursing his cotton crop for the last three years and was also responsible for his hogs, which had just recently been stricken low by some mysterious disease. The Sherwoods sued Gisburne for defamation, but ended up losing the case. At the time, witchcraft was a serious charge, and Grace could have been subject to much worse than malicious gossip if Gisburne decided to take her to court. Yet the impoverished farmer had neither the will nor the concentration to make his accusations into formal charges. He leaned toward excessive drink and constant slander. But even if the level-headed members of the community dismissed Gisburne's remarks as the drunken tirades of a desperate man, once the word "witch" was uttered Grace would never be above suspicion. And rightfully so, some would say, given the bizarre event that took place one year later.

Elizabeth Barnes was lost in a fitful sleep on a hot night late in August. She tossed and turned under the sweat-soaked sheets, murmuring unintelligible pleas at the denizens of some horrific nightmare. Her plaintive whispers became increasingly distressed until she was suddenly frightened out of sleep, her whole body tensing as if some enormous hand had mercifully yanked her from the Land of Nod. She bolted up, wide-awake in her moonlit bedroom, her face flush and her fear-filled eyes frantically searching the shadows of the room for the demons in her dream. There was nothing there—all was still. Her husband, James, was still asleep, snoring contentedly next to her, illuminated by the full moon that shone in through the window and onto their bed.

"It was just a dream," Elizabeth whispered to herself as she stared out the window and across the Virginia nightscape. "Just a dream," she repeated as she rolled out of bed and made her way across the room to where her chamber pot lay. She tried to forget the horrid images that had crowded her nightmare, consciously dwelling on daily rituals in an attempt to demystify the darkness. Try as she might, however, she couldn't put her mind at ease. Images of hostile Indians, feline monsters and slithering snakes flashed through her imagination. And then in the next instant, the darkness came to life.

She leapt out of the deep shadows in the bedroom—a tall, well-built woman wearing leather breeches, riding boots and a homespun white shirt. Elizabeth couldn't make out her face, but she was able to see the woman had dark hair piled high in a bun. She moved with incredible speed and grace; Elizabeth, too terrified to make a sound, tried to turn and run, but her movements were hopelessly slow compared to the cat-like speed of the dark-haired intruder. An instant later, Elizabeth was in the woman's clutches. The intruder grabbed Elizabeth's shoulders tightly and leapt on her back, knocking her onto the floor.

James Barnes was woken by the sound of his wife screaming. A number of ugly scenarios flashed through his mind as he jumped from bed. Were they being attacked by Indians? Was the house on fire? Was there a burglar in the house? None of these speculations could prepare James for the sight that greeted him on his bedroom floor. His wife lay prostrate, pinned to the ground by a dark-haired woman who was almost as big as he was. "What the hell is going on here!" James Barnes roared at the two struggling figures as he dashed towards the fight that his wife was obviously losing.

That was when the unspeakable occurred. The mysterious woman atop Elizabeth took one look at James Barnes and decided that this was a fight she did not want. Rolling off Elizabeth with amazing agility, she darted for the bedroom door. James made a desperate dive for the woman, catching the back of her shirt as he tumbled to the ground. But just as the intruder began to stumble, she vanished, replaced by a single black cat that appeared in mid-air. The sleek animal landed on the ground with feline ease and sped out the door in the blink of an eye. James Barnes lay winded on the floor, looking at the bedroom door in amazement. He held on to one mental image as the cat vanished from sight. It was the woman's face; she glanced at him when he rushed to the aid of his wife. For a moment, the moonlight from the window revealed her in silver-lit clarity: he swore it was the face of Grace Sherwood.

Cursing crops and hogs was one thing, but breaking into a family's home at night, attacking another settler and transforming into a black cat were altogether different.

Without fear of ridicule or reprisal, the Barneses quickly spread word of the attack throughout the community. "I'm telling you, she's as evil as she is perverse," James said to his friends over a mug of mead. "Thank God I stopped her when I did; who knows what she intended for my wife. And she has the power of the Devil on her side—I can tell you that much for certain. She turned from a woman into a cat right before my very eyes. God damn Grace Sherwood."

But it was Elizabeth's testimony that inspired fear in the local women. "She came out of the darkness, and was on me before I could even cry out," Elizabeth said through scarcely contained tears. "I don't know what she wanted from me, but she was strong, stronger than any man, and all I could see in the darkness was the white of her teeth— she was smiling the entire time."

Grace Sherwood bore the latest news in silence. She and her husband sued for defamation again, but were again unsuccessful. Many are uncertain whether the woman in the Barnes' bedroom was actually Grace Sherwood. In some accounts, Grace is written as the "Witch of Pungo," an evil woman capable of as much sorcery as the Wicked Witch of the West. In others, she is an unfortunate woman who is ostracized for her exceptional beauty, exceptional physical strength or bizarre behavior. Was Grace Sherwood a witch? Are witches imbued with magical powers? These are questions that readers must answer in accordance with their own beliefs. What can be said for sure, however, is that the majority of Grace's contemporaries believed the accusations to be true. As far as her peers were concerned, Grace was a witch.

And she was treated as one. After the event at the Barnes' home, Grace and her husband came under almost constant harassment. Their property was regularly vandalized, their children were harassed by young and old alike and all those who had previously called them friends abandoned them. For her part, Grace Sherwood endured the ridicule with remarkable stoicism. Indeed, there are some who claimed it did not bother her at all. Young pranksters who had taken to spying on the Sherwoods claimed that she had never been in better humor, and her boisterous laugh could be heard drifting across the Pungo Swamp.

That changed in 1706, when formal charges were brought against Grace Sherwood. Luke Hill and his wife, Elizabeth, accused Grace of casting evils spells on their home, causing their livestock to die and their gardens to wither. They even went so far as to say that Grace was responsible for the unseasonably dry weather in the winter of 1706.

Brought to trial on March 7 of that year, Grace pleaded innocent to the charges. But the court took Grace's long history of public suspicion into account and brought in a jury of 12 elderly women to investigate Grace's body for any marks that might indicate devil worship. It was a popular belief that witches could be identified by blemishes underneath their clothes. The idea was that the witch's body provided sustenance for creatures of the night, and birthmarks were formed on the places where witches allowed demons, imps, bats and other evil organisms to feed. The jury's investigation did not go well for Grace.

The 12 women found strange marks on her body and reported to the court that Grace was physically unlike any other woman they had seen. While this testimony was enough to damn Grace in the eyes of the local population, the county court was hesitant to pass sentence on Sherwood. The Salem Witch Trials in Massachusetts had run their controversial course about 15 years before, and judges across the country had become wary of prosecuting accused witches, lest another witch-killing frenzy break out again. Trying witches, in other words, had fallen out of judicial vogue.

Grace Sherwood's case was passed on to the Virginia Colony's Attorney General in Williamsburg, who promptly bounced it back to the court in Princess Anne County where she was originally tried. There wasn't a judge in Virginia who wanted anything to do with the Witch of Pungo. But local suspicions remained about the Hills' charge against Grace. If there indeed was a devil worshipper living among the Pungo settlers, as so many believed, then something had to be done about it.

The court decided Grace Sherwood should be put through one more test to determine if she really was a witch. On the morning of July 10, 1706, Grace was marched to the Lynnhaven River, followed by practically every inhabitant of Pungo. When they reached the banks of the Lynnhaven, Grace was stripped and bound with rope, her right thumb tied to the big toe on her left foot and her left thumb strung tightly to her right foot. The people gathered to watch the spectacle were largely unsympathetic with Grace's plight; they laughed and jeered at the naked woman, calling at the bailiffs to make sure they gave her a good toss.

Tied into a forced fetal position, Grace was picked up and, amidst the cheers of her neighbors, was tossed into the river. The test was called "ducking" or "swimming"—a bizarre procedure that had its roots in European witch trials. It was reasoned that witches, being agents of the Devil, would be rejected by any blessed or holy substance, and therefore would be forced to the surface of a body of holy water. The application of this theory involved tossing accused witches into a river or lake that had just been blessed by a priest. If a woman floated to the top, it meant that she had been rejected by the water, and was therefore guilty of being a witch. If she sank to the bottom, however, she was accepted by the spirit of God, and was not guilty of the charges made against her. The problem with the trial was its lethal Catch 22. For floating to the surface and surviving meant a guilty verdict and a consequently horrible, usually capital, punishment. But those women who sank to the bottom and were deemed not guilty of the charges against them often paid for their innocence with their lives, as many of them were pulled from the water well after they had drowned.

Grace Sherwood had no intention of waiting for Pungo residents to pull her dead body out of the Lynnhaven. Immediately going to work on the ropes the moment she was immersed in the water, Grace promptly freed herself from her constraints and swam back to shore amid the boos and hisses of the Virginians on the river-bank. But everyone gathered along the Lynnhaven River was instantly silenced when Grace stepped out of the water. They realized then that if Grace really was a witch, then she was capable of evil, and judging by the look on her face at that moment, it was obvious to all that vindication would come soon enough.

Grace stood tall on the river's edge, glowering at the assembled Virginians, a hot fire burning in her eyes. Standing naked and unashamed, she looked each one of them in the eyes, issuing a silent challenge with every glare. Minutes passed, and no one dared step forward to arrest her. There was only the sound of the rushing river and the electricity in the air, which seemed to build with each passing second. At least half the spectators became convinced that, at any moment, Grace would turn into a black cat and dash off. No such thing happened. The tension broke when two of the county officials finally approached her. She was wrapped up in a robe, bound with rope, and marched off to the county jail.

Grace Sherwood spent the next eight years in prison. There is no record of her life during this period. It could very well have been a difficult time for her. Grace's husband had died five years earlier, in 1701, so she was forced to send her three sons away to live with extended family. Many mothers would surely find such a situation difficult. But then again, Grace Sherwood was unlike any other mother in the Virginia colony. Many of the settlers in Tidewater believed that such a woman wasn't capable of maternal love. Was Grace Sherwood really an evil witch? Did she really cast spells to wreck crops, influence the weather and poison livestock? Did she transform herself into a black cat ? Or was she simply a woman who stood out in too many ways, a non-conformist at a time when conformity was one of the principal social virtues?

We will probably never know the answers to these questions, but the story of Grace Sherwood has survived to this very day. It is a prominent folktale that continues to be discussed by historians, folklore enthusiasts and those who are fascinated with the idea of the supernatural. But the fact that Grace was an accused witch isn't the only reason the latter group has taken an interest in the legend of the "Witch of Pungo."

Grace's story does not end in 1714, when she was finally released from prison, nor in 1740, when the controversial Virginian finally shook off her mortal coil. In fact, supernatural investigators claim that Grace Sherwood's story continues today, on Virginia Beach's Witch Duck Road, which runs along the banks of the Lynnhaven River.

Motorists taking Exit 2 off Highway 44 will find themselves on the road named after Grace Sherwood. Witch Duck Road ends at the Lynnhaven, passing right by the exact spot where Grace was "ducked" so many years ago. It is on this spot that numerous people driving along Witch Duck Road have seen a startling apparition that is there one moment and then gone the next.

Witnesses see her standing on the river's edge—a tall, broad-shouldered woman with dark hair, soaked to the bone and completely naked, with a dark look of unrestrained hatred on her face. Those who have seen her say that she appears as real as any living person. She is not transparent, her skin is not deathly pale, she doesn't hover above the ground and the anger in her face looks very real.

Many motorists have said that the sight of her filled them with extreme and completely irrational fear. Ostensibly a woman standing by the side of the road, she is instinctually terrifying, causing hundreds of motorists over the years to cross themselves or utter a silent prayer as they speed by the image of the solitary woman. She is usually visible from the road for only a second before cars pass the haunted site. Most motorists are glad to leave the dark-haired woman behind them.

Some, however, whose fear has been surpassed by a sense of moral obligation, ignore the fact that a naked woman standing by the side of the road is probably in need of some help. Concerned drivers have turned their vehicles around, but everyone who has gone back to the spot where the woman was standing only a few minutes previous have seen no trace of her at all.

Over the years, the woman standing by the Lynnhaven River has been spotted numerous times by people traveling on Witch Duck Road. Of course, those familiar with the local history recalled the story of Grace Sherwood almost as soon as the sightings began, and it has become accepted that she is the colonial witch who was thrown into the Lynnhaven so many years ago.

In a way, it makes sense that Grace Sherwood haunts the road that was named after her. When she emerged from the Lynnhaven after her ducking, she knew that her fate had been decided. And so she continues to haunt the spot that led to her imprisonment and to her legend. Whether she was a witch or not, Grace Sherwood seems doomed to serve an indeterminate sentence along Witch Duck Road.

The Hound on Buncombe Road

The story begins in 1850, with a humble peddler making his way up Buncombe Road, a stagecoach route that ran parallel to the modern-day I26, stretching from Charleston, on the South Carolina coast, to Asheville, North Carolina. The peddler was stopping at every town along the way, selling his wares to village folk who were, or were not, in need of cure-alls, strength potions and protective relics. He may not have been a scrupulous salesman, but what he lacked in commercial principles, he made up for with his love for animals. Indeed, there was no other animal in South Carolina that was better looked after than the man's dog. The enormous white pharaoh hound was the peddler's only friend in the world, so he doted on the beast, feeding it better food than he himself ate and keeping its pearly coat shining brightly. A great many villagers who saw the two of them walking together wondered what such an obviously impoverished man was doing with such a magnificent animal.

For its part, the hound was as intelligent and strong as it was loyal and had gotten the crooked peddler out of more than one tight situation involving throngs of dissatisfied customers and vials of liquid wart remover that were only well-packaged bottles of rosewater. With only each other to rely on, dog and master toured through much of South Carolina, living day to day with the crooked earnings the peddler made with his dubious wares.

But even the luckiest men have a finite supply of good fortune. The peddler's ran out the day he walked into the township of Goshen, South Carolina, near the Newberry County Line. A young local woman was discovered gruesomely murdered just before the time of his arrival, and the peddler and his dog were instantly the focus of the whole town's suspicions. No one wanted to believe any of their neighbors were capable of such an act, so the blame fell on the hapless newcomer, who was promptly incarcerated. The verdict was handed down before the trial began, and after a hasty one-day hearing, the poor charlatan was put to the rope.

Throughout the proceedings, the peddler's dog never left his side. It sat obediently outside the door of his jailhouse when he was waiting to be tried, walked with him to the hangman's noose and yelped piteously while he twitched on the end of the rope. Fiercely protective, the hound would have rushed to his master's aid if it was given the order. But the peddler couldn't bear the thought of anything happening to his prized animal, and gave it stern warnings to remain still throughout his incarceration and execution. Ever obedient, the dog did as it was told.

The peddler was dead for only a day when the citizens of Goshen Township decided to do something about the dog. Not budging from the spot where its master was hanged, it was heard whimpering through the entire night. The next day, it growled viciously with bared teeth and raised hackles whenever anyone approached. This carried on for three days before the locals decided to take action. Associating the hound with the purported evil of its master, they dealt with it mercilessly, forming a circle around the poor animal and pelting it to death with stones.

Locals did not know it at the time, but this act of pitiless cruelty would change the surrounding countryside forever, leading an endless stream of horrifying stories about nocturnal encounters on the stagecoach road. The sightings began soon after the dog was put to death, reported by people traveling on the stretch of Buncombe Road between Ebenezer Church in Maybinton Township, Newberry County, and Goshen Hill just across the county line.

It was described as an enormous white dog that shimmered with silvery light in the darkness, like a low wattage moon. Often people mistook their initial glimpse of the dog, puzzling at the white light moving through the trees along the road. Then it would lunge onto the path, revealing itself in its terrifying entirety. Its glistening teeth, bristling hackles and burning red eyes expressed its all too obvious intent—harm. There wasn't a single person who had to think twice about what to do. It wasn't a question of choice, but instinct, and whether the witness was on foot, on a horse or driving a carriage, a mad nocturnal chase down the South Carolina road invariably ensued.

Most people chased by the Hound of Goshen were convinced that they were running for their lives. Everything about the huge silver dog suggested bloodlust, and few who saw it lunging out of the bushes had the courage or self-possession to consider beating it back. Not that there weren't exceptions. A few men on horseback turned in their saddles and lashed at the beast with their riding crops, only to discover that their blows passed right through the dog with no effect. Many witnesses who got a close look at the shimmering canine noted that it was semi-transparent, and the surrounding foliage was vaguely visible through its ethereal coat.

Not everyone remained calm enough to observe the features of the monster that was bearing down on them. Most just turned and ran, unwilling or unable to take another look at the ungodly monster approaching. As may be imagined, witnesses on horseback or in carriages were much more fortunate than those who ran into the hound on foot. Unable to outrun the hellish white hound, pedestrians would never make it far before being overtaken by the vicious specter. The attacks that followed have been described in a number of different ways.

Some called the supernatural mauling the worst experience of their lives. Ice-cold teeth, as sharp as daggers, dug into their arms and legs and into the backs of their necks, while the ravenous animal growled and roared. These were by far the worst encounters with the Hound of Goshen, and those who suffered them usually ended up fainting in the middle of the road. They awoke a few hours later, sore and frazzled, but physically unharmed, without a single cut or slash from the nightmarish attack.

Dr. James Douglass, who owned a stately old house on a bluff overlooking the Buncombe Road, tended to more than one victim of the Hound of Goshen. They would stumble onto his property, numb and delirious, looking frantically for some sort of reprieve. Of course, Dr. Douglass, a man of medicine, was just the man to provide it, and as the 1850s progressed, he found more and more of his evenings were interrupted by casualties of the hound. Some victims were completely unconscious, brought in by nighttime travelers who had almost run them over on the road. When they were revived, these victims almost always reverted into a state of complete panic, screaming at the top of their voices and trying desperately to fight off their imaginary assailant.

Yet most cases were not so bad. Sometimes the hound was said to vanish just before it caught up with its helpless quarry. More often than not, nocturnal travelers on the Buncombe Road made the journey on horse or by carriage, and encounters with the hound left witnesses frazzled but conscious and lucid. These commuters, not too debilitated by the trauma to talk about it, were largely responsible for the spread of the Goshen Hound story.

Over the years, as the number of sightings grew and word of the spectral dog spread through South Carolina, travelers grew especially wary of the five-mile stretch of road that the hound was said to stalk. Warning was given to travelers in countless taverns and roadhouses: "If you're traveling through the night," barkeepers whispered to their patrons, "be on the watch for the hound between Ebenezer Church and Goshen Hill. Animals are scared half to death by that devilish beast."

And so people grew accustomed to the presence of the vengeful animal. Dr. Douglass, whose home was in the immediate vicinity of most of the sightings, eventually moved away, put off by the nightly arrival of traumatized travelers and the bloodcurdling howling that broke the silence of far too many evenings. Tales of the Goshen Hound continued after the Civil War and throughout the rest of the 19th century, tapering off only when the automobile replaced the horse as the dominant mode of transportation.

Sightings of the Goshen Hound from inside cars became more of a thrill than a terror, and many drivers passing through the area expected a glimpse of the legendary beast. If they were lucky, they would see a flash of white moving through the surrounding trees or spot some part of a large white dog as it loped through the bush. But it was as if the Goshen Hound itself knew that it was not as dreaded as it once was, and took to stalking the Buncombe Road less often.

Today, sightings of the Goshen Hound are rare indeed. For not only has the hound become apparently discouraged by the invincible cars rolling through its hunting grounds, but the majority of motorists now take the nearby I26, greatly reducing nighttime traffic on the Buncombe Road.

Nevertheless, travelers should be warned that individuals still testify to seeing white flashes in the trees around the old stagecoach path. Every now and then, residents in Newberry County have been woken to the sound of a horrible, high-pitched howl that couldn't possibly be made by any one of God's creatures. And to this very day, it is still strongly recommended that people do not walk the Buncombe Road at night, for while the Goshen Hound may have been thwarted by modern vehicles, people who take the road by foot are no less susceptible to attack than pedestrians 150 years ago.

Mysterious Creatures
of the Backroads

Many of us are amazed by creatures from foreign places. Behold the popularity of the local zoo. We tend to be enthralled by the platypuses, panda bears, gorillas and chimps that live within. But as far as the creatures indigenous to our home turf are concerned, not only do we grow to recognize the animals around us as a matter of course, we almost depend on the familiarity of these species to ground us to the places we call home.

For instance, a Californian would not expect to stumble upon a wild Bengal tiger while camping in Joshua Tree National Park, just as a Kansan would never dream of running into a grizzly bear while harvesting the season's crop. These animals are simply not found in these areas, and if Bengal tigers suddenly started stalking the deserts of California, a radical redefinition of the state's ecosystem would be in order.

So we might imagine the impact completely alien creatures have on people who are convinced they know the land around them. Indeed, the mere mention of fantastical beasts such as the Loch Ness Monster or the Abominable Snowman sets people's imaginations running. The question is: are these animals far more common than we believe? Are there entire species that have managed to evade the piercing gaze of humanity? And finally, do some of these creatures thrive right under our noses without our knowing?

A number of American folk stories revolve around sightings of such fantastical species lurking in the heartland.

These beasts have lived among us for centuries, but have thus far managed to avoid the rational classifications of biological science. Or perhaps it should be said that these species have nearly succeeded at avoiding detection. For every now and then they are spotted skulking through the backroads of rural America, preying on farm animals, terrorizing witnesses and striking stunned observers dumb with wonder.

FROG PEOPLE OF LOVELAND

One such species managed to stay hidden until the 1950s, when an Ohio resident of Loveland, Hamilton County, stumbled across the oddest sight in his life while driving down a local country road. There, in the middle of the wooded path, were three freakish animals that looked like something out of a B-grade science fiction movie. The man stopped his car and stared agape for a few moments, before throwing his car in reverse and tearing back to town. He was at the police station within 10 minutes.

"They were little frog people, three of them," the breathless man reported to the authorities. "They stood on two legs, about four feet tall, with arms, chests, necks, everything—except heads. Their heads were frog heads." The officer at the desk only stared incredulously, trying to fight the smile on his face.

"One of them had a stick in its hand," the man continued, "and started waving it around when he saw me. After a few seconds, sparks started shooting out the end of it. That was when I drove away."

Police made a half-hearted search through the woods around Loveland, but found no trace of the frog people described by the frantic witness. Years passed without another sighting of these creatures, and the "frog man incident" became something of a local joke, soon used as an idiom for extreme delusion or inebriation. "Are you seeing frog people yet?" a drunk man might ask another. "Don't stop now," an angry Loveland woman would respond to the ridiculous incriminations of her lover. "The frog people are on the way."

That was until March 1972, when the frog people were spotted again. This time it was the police who spotted two of the creatures. They were patrolling the rural backroads near Loveland when they came to a sudden stop, shocked at the sight of two strange creatures casually walking down the middle of the road. Reacting more out of fear than anything else, the two officers roared into town, quickly informing headquarters of their encounter.

The authorities promptly organized a search party, combing the area for the frog people. Days passed without a single sighting, and the police were about to quit the effort when a lone officer walking along Loveland Road bumped into one of the animals as it came bounding out of the bush on the side of the road. The two stood face to face for what seemed to be several long moments. The creature had brown, leathery skin and was about four feet tall. The officer would later say that it stunk to high heaven.

Without another thought, the man went for his gun. The frog bolted when the officer stumbled for his pistol and was about 10 feet away when the man opened fire. One of the bullets grazed the creature, but that was as close as the policeman got, for in the next instant it was at the banks of the Miami River. Leaping high into the air with amazing speed, the frogman dove into the river and was gone.

Although search parties combed the Loveland environs for days, they found nothing and eventually gave up. If the frog people are still around today, they've kept a low profile over the last 30 years. Some speculate that they are still seen around the area, but the locals have grown much more comfortable with them and leave the authorities out of it when they are spotted. Every now and again, rumors spread through the community of a child who steals upon a group of the frog people sunning themselves in the middle of a country road. But other than such occasional whispers, the frog people have all but vanished from Loveland. If they still dwell in Hamilton County, they are careful to avoid human detection.

THE MOTHMAN

Much has been made of the Mothman in books and movies since it was spotted on the Ohio–West Virginia border in 1966. Considered to be different things by different people, people call it an otherworldly harbinger of doom, a rare wild specimen and a product of overactive imaginations. Described as a humanoid creature standing over six feet tall with wings, an insect-like head and two burning red orbs for eyes, the Mothman first appeared on the McClintic Wildlife Sanctuary near Point Pleasant, West Virginia.

Two married couples, the Mallettes and the Scarberrys, were driving through the sanctuary when they caught sight of two burning red orbs the size of golf balls. Curious about what the objects might be, they stopped the car and peered into the bushes from inside the car. Then the twin spheres moved, and the horrified observers realized they were staring at eyeballs. An instant later, the Mothman stepped out onto the road, revealing every terrible detail of its grotesque body. Scared senseless, the witnesses tore out of the sanctuary as fast as their car could go, but the Mothman kept up with them the entire way.

Even as they hit Route 62 along the Ohio River, flying down the highway at nearly 100 miles per hour, the Mothman kept up, visible through the car's rear window, flying low to the road with easy, measured beatings of its enormous wings. The creature finally disengaged the chase when the car reached the outskirts of Point Pleasant, turning around and soaring into the dark night sky.

While many people scoffed at the reported sighting of this fantastical beast, the number of visitors to the McClintic Wildlife Sanctuary skyrocketed. People drove up and down the sanctuary roads, hoping to find a trace of the mysterious Mothman. But none of these eager curiosity seekers ever saw it. The Mothman, it seemed, was only spotted when it wanted to be—always the pursuer, never the quarry.

Soon after it was seen by the couples in McClintic, the Mothman chased a resident of Cheshire, West Virginia, down Highway 7, along the west bank of the Ohio River. The terrified driver practically buried the needle on the speedometer, but the Mothman seemed to keep up easily, visible in the man's rearview mirror as it flew low to the ground, its red eyes blazing into his through the mirror's reflection.

And then suddenly it stopped appearing, leaving the people in the region to wonder what exactly had appeared over their roads, flying after people and vehicles like a hunter in pursuit of its prey. Theories abounded about the Mothman's nature, but no one was able to come up with a satisfactory answer. Subsequent years brought occasional reports of Mothman sightings. A debate raged over 1979 sightings on the Appalachian Highway in West Virginia, in which people disagreed on the identity of a flying creature that was seen hovering over the scenic mountain drive. While many claimed that the flying creature was merely a sandhill crane, others were convinced that they had been followed by a large humanoid with wings and glowing red eyes. An oversize bird or animal aberration? Whatever the case, this was the last time appearances of the Mothman were publicly reported.

Is the Mothman ensconced in some Appalachian aerie? Has it fled to a mountainous region in another country or has it simply died? No one knows. But the memory of the creature lives on in numerous articles, books and, of course, at the box office, where the film *The Mothman Prophecies* made the creature into an otherworldly messenger. Wherever and whatever it is, the Mothman has become an enduring part of American folklore, and as with all such figures, there are many awaiting its inevitable return.

THE BEAST OF ALLEN COUNTY

It came in the night, stalking the backroads of Allen County, Ohio, during the spring of 1977, leaving a bloody trail of dead animals in its wake. It first struck on March 22,

Twenty sheep were among the many animals slaughtered by the so-called Beast of Allen County.

creeping onto a local man's farm and killing 20 of his sheep in a single attack. The predator did its nightmarish work in complete silence, so that the gruesome sight that greeted early risers was a horrible shock. It is said that when the farm's owner looked on the scene, he was thrown into a state of shock that lasted for over a month.

No one was sure what creature had wrought such destruction, but the people were determined it not happen again. There were still about two dozen sheep on the farm, and their pen was promptly fortified with heavy-duty wiring, new farm gates and six muskrat traps around the entrance. The next few nights passed without incident, but on the morning of April 26, the Ohio farmers woke to another horrendous spectacle. The wooden gates had been ripped apart, the new mesh was reduced to a tangled mess of steel wire and every single sheep in the pen had been killed, each of them lying dead in a pool of blood. All the steel traps had been sprung, but there was no trace of the immense beast responsible for wreaking this havoc.

Over the following two months, farmers all over Allen County woke to similar sights as the creature made its way through the region. One day, a farmer named Sherwood Burkholder walked into his livestock pen at first light to discover that 40 of his sheep had been killed. The next morning, the last 17 of his flock were slaughtered in the same gruesome fashion. Another farmer just south of the Burkholder property lost five sheep and his German shepherd a few days after that. By mid-May, it was estimated that over 140 sheep had been destroyed by the roving animal killer.

As for the beast itself, the first sighting of it occurred on the morning of April 28, when a woman named Maria Henderson was driving to work on Bentley Road, near the rural town of Bluffton. The sun had not yet fully risen and the light was still dim, so Henderson wasn't sure what she saw when her eyes first fell on the beast moving across the road about 30 yards in front of her. She could see that it was large and black and walked on four legs, and she thought for a moment that it might be a pony. Henderson slowed down and flicked on the high beams, hoping to get the animal off the road. It was then, under the sudden flash of the woman's headlights, that the Allen County beast revealed itself.

About half an hour later the woman described it to Bluffton police, trying hard to steady her shaking voice: a large black, cat-like animal, the size of a large dog or small pony, which leapt off the road with incredible speed when she approached it, disappearing in the blink of an eye. Similar reports followed over the spring of 1977. A large black shadow was seen darting across Allen County's back-roads late at night; more than one person going for an evening stroll cut the walk short when they noticed that they were being stalked by a pair of large green cat-eyes that shone in the night. The raids on farmers' livestock continued, reminding locals that the beast they saw on the roads at night was neither domesticated nor friendly. Soon enough, people refrained from taking any walks at night.

It was clear that the animal was making its way south. It was spotted around Bluffton in early spring, near Rockport in early April and numerous times by motorists on Highway 81 by early May. The enormous feline was near the town of Lafayette by mid-month, and was seen by Allen County residents just south of the small town on May 27. Months later, stories came in from Hardin County to the southeast about a black beast that was laying waste to farmers' livestock. After that, the mysterious animal vanished. No one ever claimed to have killed or captured it, and the memory of Ohio farmers waking up to the horrifying spectacle of a blood-soaked holding pen faded from the general consciousness. Whatever this deadly beast was, it has either ceased to be or has gone back to the place it came from.

5
Haunted Streets
and Roads

These ghosts are almost always seen in the evening hours, lurking just off the curb of some inner-city road, reliving their last moments on pathways that run by places they once called home. They are often bewildered spirits, wandering the streets under the cold urban glow of lights that were not there when they were alive. The following pages contain stories of metropolitan phantoms that haunt city roads across the land.

The Potawatomi Girl

History has forgotten her name and her story is as sad as it is short, but the faceless Potawatomi girl who met her end in northern Indiana still lives on in the local folklore more than 150 years after her death. Yet it isn't the account of her tragic demise that keeps her in the minds of so many La Porte County Hoosiers. What locals can't forget is regularly commemorated by the bizarre phenomena that occur on the spot where the young Potawatomi is believed to have passed away—the haunted corner of Tenth and I Streets in the town of La Porte, Indiana.

The dismal little chronicle begins in the winter of 1836 in the woods of southern Michigan. The Potawatomi Indians were brutally being cast out of their homes to make room for the expansion of the United States. President Andrew Jackson's policy of Indian removal, inflicted on Indians east of the Mississippi River, was in full effect, and tens of thousands of America's indigenous were forcefully removed from their traditional lands to government reservations west of the 100th meridian. Streams of people flowed west across the United States via a multitude of different roadways, forming numberless Trails of Tears for the Indians leaving their homes behind.

The nameless Potawatomi girl of this tale was only one among the exiled throng marching towards an uncertain destination. Her tribe was designated to live in what is now Osage County in the eastern part of Kansas, in a small reservation pressed against the territories granted to the Miami, Osage and Shawnee Indians. But first they had to get there.

The Indian tribes were subjected to long inhuman marches, in which men, women and children were pushed beyond exhaustion while making their way to the distant destinations selected by the federal government. Many of the elders, the young and the sick did not have the strength for such an arduous journey and never made it to the western lands they were heading for. Undernourished and overwhelmed, they died by the thousands, leaving their bones strewn all across the eastern states, north and south, from Florida to Illinois, Mississippi to Michigan— unfortunate testament to the cost of western expansion. The Potawatomi's trek was so harsh historians dubbed it the March of Death.

She had always been a delicate girl, and her parents grew concerned when she fell ill early during the first leg of their journey. Unable to walk after the fourth day of marching, she soon needed her mother, father and brothers to take turns carrying her. But they were forced to face the inevitable as their strength flagged and her illness grew worse. By the time they crossed the border into Indiana, she was almost dead. They laid her down by a seasonal watering hole the Indians called Came and Went, where she spent the last few hours of her life trying to draw tortured breaths as her mother washed her face with the shallow waters of the pond.

The pond was called Came and Went because water would fill it during the rainy season, only to evaporate completely by late summer, leaving nothing but a dried out basin. But legend has it that after the young Potawatomi died on its banks, Came and Went never filled up again. Howling winds and torrential rains would leave the basin wet and muddy, but for reasons people could never explain, the pond would never fill.

Time passed, and as the March of Death receded into the public memory, the town of La Porte—only a small cluster of cabins when the Potawatomi passed through—expanded as increasing numbers of settlers arrived in the area. The dried basin of Came and Went pond soon fell within town limits, and the resting place of the young Potawatomi girl was marked by little more than a signpost on a street corner, where Tenth Street and I Street intersected. The story of the nameless Indian girl who died on the street corner would surely have passed from the local consciousness if it wasn't for the strange and unsettling events that began to be reported there.

Some talked about the freakish cold spot that would settle over the entire intersection. Motivated by forces no one could comprehend, the cold would descend in the middle of a sweltering hot Midwestern summer day, generating a chill so extreme that pedestrians' breath would curl in clouds of vapor. Sometimes it would remain for the better part of an hour, yet on other occasions the cold would be gone within the span of a minute. There was never any warning when it would come, nor any indication of how long it would last, but the cold on Tenth and I Streets occurred enough that Hoosiers began looking for an explanation. Local old timers offered the story of the poor Potawatomi girl who was buried there before the two streets had even been paved.

Although many early residents of La Porte were skeptical of these stories, others were made into believers by the other bizarre phenomenon that occurred on the street corner. The girl was spotted by many Hoosiers, mostly at night, but often enough in broad daylight. She was a small-ish Indian girl in traditional Potawatomi garb, standing unnaturally still, as if she was a life-size, three-dimensional photograph, staring blankly at anyone who caught sight of her. All who saw the frail Indian girl standing harmlessly on the street corner were struck by a sudden wave of ter-ror. Although it was a completely irrational reaction, the seizure of fear was very real, and more than one horrified Hoosier turned and ran from the silent Indian. For those too terror-stricken to move, the girl remains visible for only a few more minutes before vanishing into thin air.

Tales of these occurrences continued until 1845, when a man named Dr. George Andrew built an impressive three-story house near the street corner. The girl's spirit then moved indoors. Residents of the house became accustomed to mysterious footsteps coming from empty parts of the house. Doors were propelled by invisible forces, violently swinging open and suddenly slamming shut right before astonished witnesses. Intense, inexplica-ble cold spots were known to form in the house, leaving shocked witnesses shivering in a profound state of unrest.

A succession of families lived in the house, but no one stayed for long; the big building often went unoccupied for many years between owners. The house had been deserted for nearly a decade when the decision was finally made to demolish it in the 1970s. In its place a medical center was built, which still stands there today. Many believe that the Potawatomi girl's ghost still lingers on in the facility, although if she does, she does not seem to be nearly as active as she once was.

Is she getting tired of dwelling over her old grave, long since forgotten by the majority of La Porte residents? Has her energy simply faded over time? Or has she finally decided to move on, down the same road her suffering people took almost 200 years ago? Perhaps she is arriving, just now, on the eastern fringes of Kansas, where the souls of her family have long waited among the blowing winds and fields of sunflowers.

Colonel Beau Hickman's Restless Spirit

He was called a "gentleman of elegant leisure and fashion," a "polished Virginian socialite who was as generous as he was refined" and a "high-spirited sporting man, always game for entertainment." Of course there were other descriptions as well. He was also dubbed "the Prince of Loafers," a "rotten con-artist" and an "ingenious sponger." Little agreement existed over the man who called himself Colonel Robert "Beau" Hickman, a professional gambler and confidence man who arrived in Washington, DC, in 1833.

He made quite an entrance into the nation's capital. Twenty years old, handsome and nattily dressed in the latest fashions, Robert rode in on an impressive chestnut sorrel, eager for action. He was sure to find it. In possession of a modest sum of cash and an abundance of charisma, Hickman enthusiastically made his rounds through the city's gambling circles. Friends came easily to

The ghost of Colonel Beau Hickman began to appear on this street corner after the National Hotel was torn down.

the flashy young man, who introduced himself as "Beau" or "the Colonel." He spent lavishly and was exceedingly generous, and it wasn't long before he was considered one of the princes of the Washington gaming scene.

No one could match Beau's enthusiasm for gambling. He was only happy if he was betting. It didn't matter if it was cards, horses, billiards or dice—the thrill of gambling never failed to get his heart going. His joy was contagious, and all who indulged in Washington's sporting scene came to believe that it was good fortune to be sitting next to the exuberant young Beau. A lucky talisman in a world where good luck was paramount, Beau commanded the highest premium for the honor of his presence. He was in high demand at every gambling table in the city, and Beau did everything he could to bless as many people as he could with his fortuitous hand.

Ironically, Beau himself wasn't the luckiest gambler around—far from it. Rarely did he win big at the tables. While many professional gamblers managed to make a tenuous living relying on systematic approaches and maybe a little bit of luck, Beau barely managed to make ends meet. He lost money consistently, giving up his losses with the same cavalier attitude with which he took in his winnings. Almost everyone assumed his carefree attitude was a sign of immense wealth. Beau didn't say anything to dispel this impression.

But in fact, the colonel was living on the edge of poverty. His natural devil-may-care demeanor and spectacular wardrobe concealed his financial straits; in truth, he had next to nothing to his name. Beau's affluence was all show, and some of his wealthiest gambling friends—who were all in on the secret—took to providing him with clandestine gifts for the privilege of his company. The colonel was never one to turn down a gift. And he always seemed to have just enough to keep up his charade of prosperity.

This was how he lived most of his life, hand to mouth, with the lion's share getting spilt on his clothes on the way up. As he got older, the meticulously dressed colonel made his headquarters in the National Hotel, a local boarding-house and watering hole on the corner of 6th Street and Pennsylvania Avenue. Years turned into decades, and by the time Beau was in his golden years, he was a member of the sporting emeriti, associating with only the most accomplished public men in the city.

And then, one day in 1873, he was gone. Having frat-ernized with so many different cliques, no one took any notice of his absence until a small obituary appeared in a daily paper, stating that their beloved Beau had recently died and been buried in a pauper's cemetery on the edge of town. No one could believe it. They were just as shocked at the colonel's death as they were surprised that he didn't have enough money for a decent burial. Glasses were raised in gambling houses all across the city, but no one felt his loss like the group of men in the National Hotel.

Celebrating the memory of the man they loved, patrons of the National Hotel were lost in the throes of sentimental inebriation by the time it was dark. They stumbled over syllables of affection and wept incon-solably at the death of such a lively man. Then, sometime past midnight, they resolved to do something about Beau's burial conditions. Indignant and charged with dis-tilled emotion, the group decided to lay him in the ceme-tery plot he deserved; they would ride out to the cemetery he was laid in, dig up his remains and rebury him in the hallowed Congressional Cemetery.

They set their plan in motion without delay. Getting their hands on a wagon, the drunken crew drove out to the dark cemetery on the edge of town, where they went from gravestone to gravestone, looking for Beau's grave. Nothing could have prepared them for what they found at their friend's resting-place. There, revealed by the shifting light of their swinging lanterns, were the soiled, stinking and slightly decomposed legs of Colonel Beau Hickman, protruding from his hastily packed burial mound. Someone had beaten them to the punch; Beau's body had already been disinterred.

Cursing the grave robbers that dared to loot the remains of their friend, the men set about digging Beau up. They soon discovered, to their horror, that the party which had beat them to the colonel's grave were not interested in taking any trinkets he may have been buried with. Theft was their game, but it was thievery of an entirely different, much more bizarre variety. The colonel had been visited by body snatchers.

The thieves had raided Beau's grave and mutilated his body, cutting out his heart and brain. Such organs sold for a fair price at medical schools across the country. This depraved class of criminals took advantage of this gruesome activity, raiding freshly buried corpses to acquire their grisly loot. Old Beau was a mess; the group of men recognized him only by his customarily fine clothes—his perfectly tailored wool pants, purple velvet waistcoat and sharp black suit jacket. Some cursed their friend's fate, others uttered a quick prayer, but all cut the delay as short as possible. Hoisting the colonel onto their shoulders, they carried him out of the cemetery and into their wagon. Without a single word, they put their whips to their horses and made their way to the celebrated Congressional Cemetery, where Beau was secretly reburied among the bodies of some of the most respected Americans in the country.

When they were finished, the enterprising crew made their way back to the National Hotel, where they killed the horror of the evening's activities with shots of whiskey. Before long, they talked their way into making light of what had just transpired, and not much later that same night, they were laughing hysterically at the gruesome absurdity of the entire operation. "At least," they reasoned with desperate laughter, "we gave the colonel the burial he deserved."

There is reason to believe, however, that Beau did not find his postmortem adventure to be quite so amusing. After that night, Beau's old friends began to experience strange things when they were at the National Hotel. While at the card tables, many of them often felt something like ice-cold breath blowing down the backs of their necks. Shivering to the bone, these men would throw frightened glances over their shoulders, but never saw anything that could explain the frigid drafts. Others claimed that they occasionally heard Beau's voice whispering advice when dwelling over bets. Those that took the mysterious voice's advice unfailingly lost their money. None of the men who participated in the colonel's reburial ever felt comfortable in the National Hotel again. They became convinced that their jovial old friend's spirit was not at all happy about what happened to his remains. Thanks to the loquacious nature of these boisterous card players, the story of Beau's unhappy spirit became news about town, and the colonel quickly became as famous in death as he was in life.

If it was indeed true that the ghost of Beau still frequented his old headquarters, he wasn't able to stay there for long. In 1892, the National Hotel was torn down to make way for the new headquarters of the Atlantic Coastline Railroad, leaving the ghost of the colonel without a gambling house to haunt. But that wasn't the final word on Colonel Beau Hickman.

Soon after the National Hotel was torn down, a strange old man began to be spotted on the corner of 6th Street and Pennsylvania Avenue. He only appeared at night, and was usually described in the same way: standing with his back to traffic, staring up at where the old hotel used to be. Sharply dressed in a black suit and purple velvet waistcoat, the man looked stately but mournful, with an almost wistful expression discernible on his face through the streetlights. People on horses or in carriages were often stricken by how still the man was as he stood there, and they would slow down to ask if he needed any direction. As soon as he was addressed, he would vanish into thin air.

Word of the vanishing old man quickly spread through the city, and it wasn't long before people pegged him as none other than Colonel Beau Hickman, the dear old gambler who died without a penny in his pocket and who was buried twice, once by the church, and once by the best of Washington's sporting men. It was surmised that even death hadn't cured him of his gambling habit, and he still returned to the site of his old haunt in the hope of finding a good card game. Of course, he's had no luck since the National Hotel was demolished, and so his lost soul stands there uncomprehending, gazing longingly at where his ersatz home used to stand.

To this very day, motorists driving by the corner of 6th and Pennsylvania late at night have claimed to see an old man in a startlingly old-fashioned suit, walking up and down the sidewalk. He is said to look bewildered and lonely, scanning the surrounding buildings and gazing up and down the street for someone or something familiar. Newcomers in town often stop and ask him if he needs any help getting anywhere, whereupon the man vanishes right before their eyes. But those cabbies and bus drivers accustomed to the city and its environs don't even slow down at the sight of him. When passengers ask them to stop for the obviously lost old man, their response is always the same. "Nah, that's just the ghost of the colonel, and it's pretty well impossible to take him where he needs to go."

A Regretful Spirit on First Street

Joseph Holt was never a popular man. Born with a dour disposition and vindictive personality, he never bothered much with anything that was unrelated to money or personal advancement. In these pursuits, at least, he was extraordinarily talented. Holt was a master of systems and analysis, famous for his abilities at organization and management. Yet when it came to managing any other aspect of his life, Holt was a mess. He was a quiet man who only spoke when he had something especially vicious to say, and no one who knew him could ever say that they saw him smile. He went through his life completely unaffected

Some speculate that the ghost of Joseph Holt continues to be obsessed with the outcome of the Lincoln assassination trial.

by the finer things, motivated almost entirely by personal ambition and bitter rancor.

Although Joseph Holt never had many friends, he did manage to ascend the ladder of professional achievement, winning the most prestigious appointments in the United States' federal bureaucracy. He arrived in Washington, DC, in 1857 to work as a commissioner in the government's Patent Office. The next five years saw his rapid advancement through the government machinery, during which time he went from Commissioner of Patents to Postmaster General to Secretary of War. Eventually he became the country's first Judge Advocate General of the United States Army.

It was Holt's work in this last capacity that would cast his name into the annals of American history. Appointed in 1862, he was the judge who presided over the Lincoln assassination trial in 1865. As the leading official of the military commission that oversaw the case, he ended up sentencing four of the convicted conspirators to the gallows—Lewis Paine, George Atzerodt, David Herold and, most memorably, Mary Surratt. While the dutiful Holt managed to remain aloof of the public furor surrounding the case, he never fully recovered. If he was a difficult man before, he became downright malignant after the trial. Becoming susceptible to sudden bursts of violent temper, Holt completely shut himself off from the world around him. When he wasn't poring over his desk at work, he was holed up in the parlor of his Capitol Hill home, on First and C Streets, slouched before a roaring fire, staring blankly into the blaze, lost in some dark and mysterious rumination.

The cause of Holt's endless rumination was not much of a mystery to Washington society. It was believed that the execution of Mary Surratt had left an ugly blot on his conscience. Was Surratt's involvement a fatal misunderstanding or murderous scheming? This dark question hung over the entire Lincoln assassination trial and helped to turn Joseph Holt inward on himself. In the dark confines of his shuttered sitting room, he brought all his prodigious analytical talents to face the demons of his murderous soul.

Mary Surratt kept the boardinghouse where John Wilkes Booth stayed while scheming against President Lincoln. At the trial, she was considered guilty by association. Arguing that Surratt was an active member of the assassination conspiracy, the prosecution brought forward witnesses who testified to her involvement in the nefarious plot. But the testimony was weak, and later it became clear that the witnesses who provided it had testified under undue coercion, rendering most of their statements false. Nevertheless, the Military Commission found her guilty of conspiracy to commit murder, and she was set to face sentencing alongside Paine, Atzerodt and Herold. While there was no question these three men were going to face the death penalty, there was some question over the fate of Surratt.

Not only was the testimony against her shaky, but she was also a woman; the conventions of the time did not readily allow a woman to be sentenced to death. As such, the commission that tried her recommended to President Andrew Johnson that she be shown mercy "due to her sex and her age," and there were few who really expected her to be hanged. The question of why she was hanged in the end eventually became a serious issue of contention between Joseph Holt and Andrew Johnson.

Holt was publicly vilified soon after Mary's death, accused of suppressing evidence that may have led to her exoneration and even keeping the Military Commission's plea for clemency from Andrew Johnson. President Johnson even went public, saying that he wasn't given the

*Conspirators in the Lincoln assassination were hanged on June 7,
1865; Mary Surratt is on the far left.*

plea when Holt handed over the court transcripts and
deliberation. Holt claimed the opposite, countering that
he had explicitly informed the president of the commission's request, but Johnson went ahead and ordered her
execution along with the three other conspirators.

No one knows for certain who was telling the truth, but
it is largely believed that the depression Holt fell into soon
after the trial was a result of Surratt's execution. Acutely

aware of the accusations that were being leveled at him, he offered a public rebuke in 1866, publishing a pamphlet that condemned all opposition to his verdict as treasonous slander. It was backed by none other than Jefferson Davis, former president of the Confederacy. But the pamphlet came across as delusional babble more than anything else, and Holt's neighbors and associates recognized its issuance as his first step down the road to madness.

Holt's manner declined quite dramatically after the trial. His temper had made him difficult to work with before, but after 1865 it became shorter and more volatile. His appearance at work began to alarm his colleagues. He grew extremely pale, developing dark purple circles under his miserable eyes, in which some observers noticed traces of something they had never seen before: fear. He lost weight, looked disheveled and acquired the disturbing habit of mumbling to himself in public.

But it was after he resigned as Judge Advocate General in 1875, a full decade after Mary Surratt was executed, that Joseph Holt's ties to reality were completely broken. From the day he stepped down from public office, he was seen by few. Sequestering himself in the house on First Street, Holt let his mind fall into the proceedings of the long-concluded trial, reading the transcripts over and over again until he could recite the entire proceedings by heart. He let his home go as well; the weeds and grass grew thick and high in his yard, climbing over the crumbling walls of his decaying home. And although his neighbors had always tried to be friendly, they now cast suspicious glances at the overgrown lot, muttering angrily among themselves of the "unconscionable judge" whose presence on their block was a moral and visual blot.

The years came and went, and the neighborhood children made up all sorts of stories—gory, frightening and fantastical—to explain the presence of the dramatically decaying house. Most of the stories revolved around one bold child's foray into Holt's home. Upon entering a darkened room that was thick with dust and spider webs, the boy saw an ancient skeleton of a man sitting staring wide-eyed into a book that lay open in his lap. The child wasn't sure if he was alive or dead until the old man slowly turned his head to glare at the young interloper, staring for a few seconds before emitting a hideous roar of unfathomable anger.

Somehow, Holt managed to hold onto life for nearly 20 more years, finally passing away on August 1, 1894. Nearby residents tried to erase every sign of the bitter old man's presence after his passing, and the house's next residents tried to breathe new life into the place by cleaning up the yard, painting the house and renovating the interior. But they did not stay long in the house. No one, in fact, who lived in Holt's former home remained for long. They all emerged with eerie accounts of strange sights and sounds that occurred within. Some heard the sound of footsteps slowly making their way across the wooden floor, while others heard the sound of a crackling old voice, speaking in the evenly timed cadence of a man reading out loud. A select few were unfortunate enough to catch sight of a grimly emaciated old man trudging through the halls.

Word of the ghost in Holt's old residence spread through the city, and the derelict house was finally torn down after being empty for years. It was then, when the former judge's old abode was demolished, that Joseph Holt finally started to make his rounds through the streets of Washington, DC, again.

He began appearing near the turn of the century. A hopelessly skinny old man walking down First Street late at night, he muttered incessantly to himself while huddled deep within a dark Union cloak. Those who saw the old man briskly making his way towards Capitol Hill with his painfully lopsided gait instantly knew there was something wrong. They felt it in their bones: the emaciated man shambling through the darkness was something more, or less, than human.

Various people reacted differently to the strange, somehow frightening sight of the old man in the darkness. Some thought it odd that this elderly man should be walking the streets at such a late hour. They called out to him, stopping on the sidewalk, pulling their horses to a stop, signaling their carriage drivers to pull up next to him, or, later on in the century, slowing down their cars to drive alongside him. Yet anyone who tried to communicate with him was in for the shock of a lifetime. The moment he was addressed, the man would vanish into thin air, remaining visible only long enough to cast a withering glare at the person who had interrupted his manic musing.

Although this disappearing act was disquieting to those who witnessed it, something much more horrifying was in store for pedestrians who said nothing to the old man as he approached. Those unfortunates who have gotten close enough to make out snippets of the mysterious man's speech say that he speaks in an eerily measured rhythm, as if reciting something he has read and repeated countless times over. Most people have described his words as legal jargon spoken too quickly to be intelligible, but others have been able to make out strings of sentences: "I hereby acknowledge the service of the writ hereto attached and return the same, and respectfully say that the body of Mary E. Surratt is in my possession…" or "During the winter and spring, and up to the night of the assassination, I boarded with Mrs. Surratt. While there I…" Those who are able to make out the man's words usually only hear a few sentences before they are overcome by a sickening stench of rot that hits them when the man is about arm's length away.

The odor has been likened to a repugnant bouillabaisse of death and animal refuse. Many have claimed the smell was so intense that they became temporarily incapacitated, doubling over as the old man shuffled past them. They regain their breath and look about frantically for the man who visited such agony upon them. Yet there is never any sign of him on either side of First Street. Their watery eyes serve as the only evidence that he was ever there at all.

As the number of sightings increased, people began putting the pieces together. The old man's words were from the transcript of Mary Surratt's trial, and although no one has seen any photographs of Joseph Holt, the nocturnal pedestrian on First Street has been likened to a withered version of the Judge Advocate General who scowls at the cameras in surviving photographs. There is also the matter of the specter's recurring appearance on the same stretch of road: First and C Streets, the address of the late Joseph Holt's home.

To this day, sightings of this frightening old man continue to be reported by late-night drivers and pedestrians on First Street. Clad in his long Union jacket, the tall and spindly old man moves spastically on bone-thin legs, gesturing wildly in the air in front of him as he goes through the court proceedings that saw an innocent woman hanged. Whether he is festering with a guilty conscience or simply looking for a home that no longer stands is not known for certain. Yet if pedestrians find themselves approaching an old man that matches his description while walking down First Street late at night, they might think twice before approaching what could very well be the ghost of Joseph Holt, who seems just as talented at repulsing people in death as he did in life.

Outrun the Devil

Captain Abram Simons was probably aware of the contradictions in his life. A leading member of the community in Washington, Georgia, during the early 19th century, Simons rose to prominence on the basis of his roadside tavern just outside of the town, on Washington Road. Although his business provided food and drink for travelers coming and going in and out of town, most of Captain Simons' profits came from the more controversial commerce of the sporting world. For Simons' Inn was also a gambling house, a bustling one at that, and the old

Phantom hoofbeats are the spectral remnants of Captain Abram Simons' unusual attempts to outrun the Devil.

Revolutionary War captain made a hefty sum banking on other men's vices.

Simons' Inn provided for almost every gambling preference. If men wanted to bet on cards, he had multiple games going in his common room. Dice? A number of primitive craps tables dotted his establishment. And for those who wished to see their gambling dollars put into more physical contests, Simons had a racetrack and stables built behind his inn, providing a venue for betting on horses.

Yet despite his immoral business, Simons' conscience was largely shaped by Christian belief. His wife was a religious woman, and Simons himself made it a point to go to mass every Sunday at Smyrna Church, just down the street from Simons' Inn. Of course, this disagreement between ideals and action created a fair bit of tension in Simons' mind, and he rarely fared well when the Smyrna minister paid him a visit trying to convert him to the righteous path.

"You're living a life of sin, Abram," the preacher would say, "and there's gonna come a time, when no matter how fast the horses in your stable are, you'll never ride fast enough to outrun the Devil."

"C'mon now Father," Abram would respond with a lopsided grin, giving his best attempt at meekness. "I'm just a simple man trying to make a living. There's no need to call down the thunder."

"You make your so-called 'living' on other men's sins," the preacher would offer back, "and when the Final Day of Reckoning is at hand, you'll see that this isn't a living, never was. In fact, your soul's been dying all along."

Sometimes these conversations went on for a long time, with the pastor trying everything he could to convince Abram of the error of his ways, while the barkeeper disguised his religious anxiety underneath a thin veneer of cockiness. But the exchanges would always end the same, with the preacher leaving in a frustrated huff and Abram Simons secretly nursing a consuming concern over the ultimate fate of his soul. Yet despite his trepidation,

Abram never once considered changing his ways. In fact, it is written in local folklore that Abram became increasingly unscrupulous in his elder years, engaging in blatantly unethical business practices to keep the money coming in. According to some accounts, he even had servants bring buckets of water up from Upton Creek, soaking the packed dirt of Washington Road in front of his tavern. This turned it into a muddy slough that no wagon, carriage or buggy could navigate through. Forced to wait until the road dried, the teamsters would end up spending the night at Simons' Inn, spending their money on food, drink and entertainment.

Business boomed and the years brought considerable wealth to the Washington innkeeper; but the richer he got, the more tortured his conscience became. The local priest's sermons grew more forceful with every visit, and Abram was soon fixated on one of the priest's favorite metaphors for damnation: being chased by the Devil. He envisioned his spiritual life as a physical race against Satan and began to prepare himself for the contest.

As he grew older, more and more of Simons' waking hours were spent perfecting his riding. He began on his racetrack. Locals would spy him on the track, racing his fastest horse, Babylon, on endless laps, not quitting until his horse was foaming at the mouth and near collapse. Before long, Simons graduated to the surrounding forest, taking to Washington Road with the same zeal reserved for drunks and madmen. He became a common hazard to commuters traveling along the thoroughfare, tearing around corners and over straightaways on the dirt road with reckless abandon. "Be extra careful traveling

Did a priest's powerful sermons inspire Captain Simons to race along Washington Road?

Washington Road late at night or early in the morning," locals would say. "That's when ol' Abram's on the road, practicin' up for the day he has to outrun the Devil."

More than one traveler almost collided with Abram Simons on the Wilkes County road. The only warning they were given of his approach was the sound of Babylon's hooves pounding on the packed dirt; in the next second Abram was on them, hooves, shouts, neighing horses and creaking wheels forming a harrowing promise of collision. Only quick reactions and luck, tested time and again, averted certain disaster.

These near-death experiences and Abram's best times on Washington Road became the sole subjects of conversation at the Simons' dinner table. It got so bad that Abram's wife visited the Smyrna Church priest and begged him to use a different analogy for damnation. "You don't understand, Father," she said. "Abram's not the kind of man who'll back down from a challenge. You've got him thinking about Judgment Day like it's a race no one thinks he can win. Well, he's dead determined to prove to us all that he can beat the odds. And at this point, I'm curious about how fast the Devil really rides, Father, because I'm willing to tell Abram that he just topped Lucifer if that gets him off the road. He's scaring everyone in town to death and has near killed himself over a dozen times."

But as men of God are wont to be, the Smyrna Church pastor was firm in his convictions. He allowed no debate about the ultimate ends of Abram's sinful ways and refused to tell the innkeeper that he and his horse were now fast enough to outrun the ramifications of his actions in the afterlife. For his part, Abram never did get in the lethal road accident that his wife feared. Against all the odds, Abram lived into old age, naturally succumbing to the weight of his years in 1824, with his wife and priest at his bedside. But he did not die peacefully. His upcoming race with the Devil was nigh, and he affirmed that he was ready for the contest, but his favorite horse, Babylon, was still a strong and healthy animal, with at least another decade of life in its muscular limbs. "What am I going to do, Father?" Abram croaked from his deathbed. "My fastest horse still has many years to live. I don't have a mount to bear me away from the Devil."

"Repent," the priest replied, "and you may still be saved."

But Abram was a stubborn man who was proud of his worldly accomplishments and had a great deal of difficulty putting faith in anyone or anything besides himself. He ignored the priest's counsel, then turned to his wife and said, "These are my last wishes. Do not bury me in the church cemetery, but on top of the knoll behind our inn. The church cemetery is surrounded by trees, and I want to have the high ground so I can see the Devil coming well before he gets to me. Also, I want to be put into the earth standing up, with a musket by my side, so I can take a shot at him if he gets too close. Maybe I'll be able to keep him back long enough for Babylon to join me."

He died with this request fresh on his lips. Mrs. Simons honored his last wishes, burying him at the top of the hill on their property, standing up with a loaded musket by his side. Time passed and travelers got used to a safer Washington Road, without the galloping peril of crazy old Abram Simons to worry about. Mrs. Simons remarried a man who assumed ownership of the inn; Babylon, deprived of its daily runs through the forest, grew slow and indolent in its later years. The priest of Smyrna Church took to using the story of Simons as the model of a damned man, pointing to Abram's stables and bellowing: "There, feeding on hay, is the savior of the vain sinner."

And so Abram Simons passed from the world of the living, slowly receding from local memory as the years passed, becoming nothing more than a deceased eccentric who was brought up in reminiscence. More than his wife or his tavern, people associated the old man's memory with Babylon, his favorite steed, now an old nag relegated to pulling wagons and menial duties. Simons would have surely faded into obscurity if it wasn't for the bizarre events that began to occur soon after Babylon died.

Simons' horse died without notice; the death of a worn-out beast of burden was hardly an event worth commemorating, and no one could have known that Babylon's dying breath would inaugurate the haunting of Washington Road. It is impossible to guess today the identity of the first Georgian who dove off the road at the sound of thundering hooves approaching out of the darkness, yet this frightened commuter would be the first among many to witness Abram Simons' return from the grave.

Not that anyone actually saw the old tavern owner. The phantom rider galloped down Washington Road only late at night, well after the sun had set, or in the early morning when the first sunlight broke through the woods. Commuters would hear the hooves beating upon the road so vigorously that the sound was as much felt as it was heard. It was as if some unknown rider had come out of nowhere, but was now so close that there was bound to be a collision if someone didn't act fast. Riders sent their mounts crashing into the surrounding woods, dived off their mounts or stood dumbstruck, frozen in the face of the impending accident. Yet nothing ever happened; there was no rider, no galloping horse, no fatal collision. The sound of the hooves on packed dirt got louder for an instant longer, then faded into the trail behind them, as if an invisible horse and rider had just run by at a speed too great to imagine.

On the verge of being forgotten, Abram Simons was suddenly looming in the public consciousness again. Locals connected the phenomenon on Washington Road to Abram's old riding routine, and it was soon surmised that perhaps it was his spirit, finally reunited with his favorite horse, that was tearing down the rural pathway again. If so, were horse and master still practicing for their long-anticipated race with the Devil? Or had Abram Simons actually held off the Devil for the decade that Babylon outlived him, and was now engaged in the race of his life? If Washington residents considered either theory fanciful, at least they provided explanations for a baffling phenomenon, which, believe it or not, continues to be reported by Washington residents and travelers alike.

Today there is no longer any trace of Abram Simons' inn, and the pathway he spent so many years racing down has been renamed South Smyrna Church Road. Yet little about the road itself has changed. Still unpaved, it remains a hard dirt road winding through the woods just outside the town of Washington. Compared to nearby Highway 78, the road gets very little traffic, and there are few living close enough who are able to hear the sounds of a phantom horse's hooves.

Yet there still are Georgians residing near the former location of Simons' Inn; and there still are some motorists whose daily destinations take them down South Smyrna Church Road. Residents and motorists have both heard the hooves on the road. Some have been woken in the middle of the night by the sound of the galloping horse, while others have brought their vehicles to sudden stops at the sound of the approaching animal that never comes. And so it seems that Abram Simons is still making his frantic supernatural getaway from a swift Lucifer, galloping down South Smyrna Church Road as fast as Babylon can carry him.

The Ghosts of Clark Street

Compared to any other urban stretch of road in North America, Chicago's Clark Street must certainly be ranked near the top for ghostly activity. Intersecting two of Chicago's greatest disasters, Clark Street runs north-south straight through the city center, stretching through Printer's Row, The Loop, over the Chicago River and into the Near North. It is one of the bustling city's busiest streets, teeming with traffic throughout the daylight hours and into the dusk, still busy well after the sun goes down. For Chicagoans swept along in the rush of city life, Clark Street is just another expanse of concrete through which the pulse of the city flows. Tourists are encouraged to walk down Clark Street for a glimpse of "the real Chicago," as it is at work and at play.

There is another side of Clark Street, however, that is largely disregarded by the local urbanites and tourist brochures. Perhaps it is ignored for the same reason that dead bodies are promptly covered by authorities at the scene of the crime and corpses displayed in open caskets are made up to look as life-like as possible. The fact is that we, as a people, have difficulty staring into the face of death and tend to ignore it for as long as we possibly can.

On Clark Street, death holds high dominion. Although the matter is largely ignored, dismissed or laughed at by the living, the immense loss of life that has occurred just off the central Chicago street during the last century has left an indelible mark. It may not be obvious to casual observers, and has largely been overlooked by those who espouse the rational, forward-looking spirit of the times, but the Clark Street dead have found a way to whisper into the cacophony of life in the Windy City.

They were two separate incidents: one a tragic disaster in 1915, resulting in the deaths of hundreds of innocents; the other an infamous 1929 gangland murder that left seven thugs dead against a warehouse wall. Both events occurred along Clark Street and both resulted in a slew of inexplicable sights, sounds and stories that have been witnessed and repeated by succeeding generations. These are the ghost stories of Clark Street, the tales of the bitter dead who are taken before their time.

When the *Eastland* quietly tipped into the Chicago River on the morning of July 24, 1915, no one present could have guessed the scope of the disaster. Loaded with about 3000 Western Electric employees, the clumsy steamer had barely disembarked from its moorings when it began to list badly to the port side. The *Eastland* always had the tendency to tip; it was a narrow boat, dangerously top heavy, with a skeleton crew. But on that July morning, Captain Harry Pedersen had allowed the ship to be stuffed well above capacity. The *Eastland* had a carrying capacity of about 2500 passengers, but Captain Pedersen obviously didn't worry too much about the short journey to Michigan City, Indiana, where the

Today, screams and painful cries serve as ghostly reminders of the
Eastland's *tragic sinking in Chicago on July 24, 1915.*

Western Electric employees were planning to have their
annual company picnic.

The journey had barely begun when Pedersen realized
how wrong he was. Almost instantly, the ship began to list
to the port; the captain took all the measures that could
be expected of him to correct the problem. He ordered
the starboard ballast tanks to be filled, hoping to compen-
sate by adding weight to the opposite side of the boat.

When the *Eastland* continued to tip towards the left side, he ordered passengers on the ship deck to move to the starboard rail. But even with all the passengers on deck leaning against the right rail, the ship continued to list. Crawling up the Chicago River, the *Eastland* was practically right up against the Clark Street Bridge when it finally tipped over into the water.

It happened in a matter of minutes. At one moment, the steamer was listing at a dangerous angle; the next, it was floating on its side in the water, among hundreds of people thrashing in the river. They were the lucky ones, the passengers who had been on deck when the *Eastland* tipped over. For the people below deck the steamer was instantly transformed into a deathtrap. Stuck within rooms that were rapidly filling with water, many of the passengers down below lived their last moments banging against the inside of the hull in a desperate plea for help.

Some of them received it. As soon as the ship went down, rescue workers rushed to the scene, punching holes into the ship's hull and pulling whomever they could reach out of the flooding rooms. Yet for most of those on the lowest levels of the *Eastland*, rescue was actually recovery, and by the time all was said and done, over 835 corpses had been pulled from within the ship and off the river bottom. Like most great disasters, the *Eastland* incident did not vanish into history the moment the bodies were buried. One of Chicago's greatest tragedies, it was lived and relived over the decades, becoming the subject of countless lawsuits. Commemorated with a plaque, the site of the tragedy also became the home of the ghosts of Clark Street Bridge.

They were first reported by Clark Street pedestrians shortly after the disaster—horrible screams, cries of pain, mournful wails. They were heard all along Clark Street Bridge, drifting up from the Chicago River, sending chills of fear down some witnesses' spines, causing others to break into uncontrollable tears. Some were even sent into fearful dashes off the overpass. Those who have quelled their fear and looked over the edge of the bridge to catch sight of the distressed parties are only greeted by the sight of the Chicago River as it slowly moves east—completely deserted, without a soul to be seen in the water or along the banks.

The terrible sounds on Clark Street Bridge have survived the passage of years, becoming one of the city's most recognized supernatural phenomena. But as such, the cries off the river have always been brushed aside by skeptics and authorities alike, who have always offered a number of alternate, more rational, explanations for the source of the sounds. But if these distressed voices do belong to the souls lost on the *Eastland*, some of the boat accident casualties have not limited their after-death activities to wailing in the dark.

She has been spotted intermittently over the years, first appearing exactly one month after the *Eastland* tragedy, shrouded in a heavy gray cowl with the deep hood drawn up and hands tucked into the sleeves. She walks slowly across Clark Street Bridge at night, moving with an odd, unnatural gait, her legs barely moving under her robe as she makes her way forward, almost making it look as if she is floating, rather than walking over the bridge. Witnesses claim to have been seized by a constricting sense of fear, rendered unable to think of anything apart from getting as far away from the mysterious figure as possible. This is never a difficult task, for the woman walks very slowly, disappearing the moment she gets to the end of the bridge. No one knows who she is or why she continues to make her nocturnal walk across Clark Street Bridge. All that is certain is that she made her first appearance on August 24, 1915, and was spotted by Chicagoans throughout the 20th century. According to eyewitnesses, she still appears to this day, making her slow march across the bridge. She is illuminated only by the cold electric streetlights, looking nowhere but straight ahead, either completely unaware of or totally unimpressed by Chicago's changing cityscape. Is she an angel of grief, eternally mourning the immense and meaningless loss of life in the waters below? Or is she some sort of visual manifestation of death itself, revisiting the site that relegated so many to their watery graves? We may never know.

The victims of the *Eastland* disaster aren't the only specters from the city's past that haunt Clark Street. Farther north along the old Chicago thoroughfare lurk the ghosts of one of the city's most infamous murders. The St. Valentine's Day massacre shocked the city and the country on February 14, 1929. One of the most sensational gangland hits in American history, the murder was engineered by Jack McGurn, one of Al Capone's most vicious killers. The attack was intended to deliver the coup de grace to Capone's number one underworld competitor, Bugs Moran.

The hit took place on a brisk winter morning, at about 10:30 AM. Seven of Moran's associates were in the S.M.C. Cartage Company garage on 2122 Clark Street, waiting for whiskey smugglers who were supposed to arrive at any moment. But not only were their suppliers late, their boss, Bugs Moran, who was supposed to be handling the cash for the transaction, was also late. These concerns quickly dissolved when four police officers suddenly burst into the warehouse.

"Alright you crooked louses," one of the plain-clothes officers roared into the cavernous warehouse, "this is a raid, and if you know what's best for you, you'll line up against that wall, backs to me."

The men hesitated.

"Pronto," he yelled again, his voice echoing in the garage.

Two of the police were in uniform, armed with shotguns that were leveled at the gangsters, and the other two were plain-clothes officers brandishing wicked-looking tommy guns. Moran's boys had to concede that they'd been beaten; none of them had seen this coming. *A raid,* thought Pete Gusenberg, one of Moran's men. *So who the hell's the rat?* This would be his last thought.

A moment later, the sound of gunfire exploded within the warehouse as the men dressed as police officers opened up on the backs of their rivals. Tommy-gun fire and shotgun blasts tore through the room for the better part of a minute, leaving the seven men lying in a gory pool against the warehouse wall. The hitmen then walked out of the garage as quickly as they came, with the two uniformed killers leading their plain-clothed associates out by gunpoint, so that it would look to witnesses as if the gunfight within the garage had led to the arrest of the two suited men. They got into their police car and tore down Clark Street. None of the killers was ever apprehended.

Although Capone rival Bugs Moran survived the St. Valentine's Day attack, his gang suffered an irreversible blow.

The men were mobsters on Al Capone's payroll, and the infamous hit broke the power of Moran's North Side gang. Of course, it carried other ramifications as well. Until then, the people of Chicago had always been strangely sympathetic of the charismatic Capone, but the horrible crime on Clark Street turned the public against the mobster. Law enforcers in Washington, DC, viewed the massacre as

Chicago's nadir and commissioned Elliot Ness and his band of Untouchables to solve the Capone problem.

Such a brutal massacre left behind psychic residue. This factor probably didn't enter the hitmen's minds at the time, and it is a notion that is probably scoffed at by most of the hardened men that live by the gun. However, it has been said that during his later years, Al Capone was haunted by the ghosts of some of the men he had killed; indeed, many believe that the spirit of James Clark, one of the St. Valentine's Day victims, was what expedited the legendary mobster's descent into madness. Hundreds of motorists who have driven down North Clark Street late at night attest to the truth of Capone's demons.

The warehouse turned into something of a local attraction after the massacre, becoming the destination for countless tourists and curiosity seekers around the world. They all came to see and touch the wall that Moran's men were shot against. Even 20 years later, when the garage was turned into a furniture shop, most of the people who walked through the doors were not there to buy furniture, but to see the famous wall. It wasn't until 1967, when the old building was demolished, that the strange sounds began to be heard along North Clark Street.

They were reported by late night motorists: gunshots, machine gun fire, cries of pain, sharp and clear, as if a gunfight had suddenly erupted right over Clark Street. Some drivers have been so startled that they almost swerved off the road in panic, convinced that they were being shot at. The police have been summoned to the area on more than one occasion, but they have never discovered any evidence of an exchange of gunfire. No shell

Many paranormal phenomena have been reported near the warehouse where the St. Valentine's murders occurred.

casings, blood stains or discarded firearms have ever been found to support the reports of a shootout.

Although many have simply chosen to leave the incident unexplained, other people, particularly those who have actually heard the sounds of gunfire on the road, have felt impelled to look a little deeper into the phenomenon. No one who has done any sort of research on the area can ignore that the biggest gangland hit in the history of the city took place right on that very stretch of Clark Street. Of course, the proximity of the St. Valentine's Day massacre to the sounds of gunfire raises more questions than it answers.

If these shots actually are somehow associated with the killings that took place so many years ago, why does the gunfire from this massacre continue to be heard today? What is it about the St. Valentine's Day murders that has caused the gunshot sounds to linger on over the decades? Are they a guilty expression made by the remorseful souls of the killers? Souls who are tortured to linger over Clark Street until they pay whatever price is asked of them? Or perhaps they are manifestations of the seven victims, whose spirits still haven't gotten over the violent sudden-ness of their deaths.

In any case, motorists best beware when they are mak-ing their way north on Clark Street. They are on a road that runs through two of the city's most infamous events—a road that is said to be haunted by the ghosts of both the *Eastland* steamer and the St. Valentine's Day massacre. These ghosts are forever stuck on the side of the road, repeatedly revisiting their deaths as the traffic of the living rushes by.

THE END